What I Learned and What I Learnt

ABOUT THE CRITICAL BLACK PEDAGOGY IN EDUCATION SERIES

The Critical Black Pedagogy in Education Series highlights issues related to the education of Black students. The series offers a wide range of scholarly research that is thought-provoking and stimulating. It is designed to enhance the knowledge and skills of pre-service teachers, practicing teachers, administrators, school board members, and higher education employees as well as those concerned with the plight of Black education. A wide range of topics from K–12 and higher education are covered in the series relative to Black education. The series is theoretically driven by constructs found in cultural studies, critical pedagogy, multicultural education, critical race theory, and critical White studies. It is hoped that the series will generate renewed activism to uproot the social injustices that impact Black students.

Other Books in the Critical Black Pedagogy in Education Series
Multicultural Education for Educational Leaders: Critical Race Theory and Antiracist Perspectives, edited by Abul Pitre, Tawannah G. Allen, and Esrom Pitre
Education Leadership and Louis Farrakhan, by Abul Pitre
Living the Legacy of African American Education: A Model for University and School Engagement, edited by Sheryl J. Croft, Tiffany D. Pogue, and Vanessa Siddle Walker

What I Learned and What I Learnt

Teaching English While Honoring Language and Culture at a Predominantly Black Institution

Concetta A. Williams
Lydia Brown Magras

ROWMAN & LITTLEFIELD
Lanham • Boulder • New York • London

Published by Rowman & Littlefield
An imprint of The Rowman & Littlefield Publishing Group, Inc.
4501 Forbes Boulevard, Suite 200, Lanham, Maryland 20706
www.rowman.com

6 Tinworth Street, London SE11 5AL, United Kingdom

Copyright © 2019 by Concetta A. Williams and Lydia Brown Magras

All rights reserved. No part of this book may be reproduced in any form or by any electronic or mechanical means, including information storage and retrieval systems, without written permission from the publisher, except by a reviewer who may quote passages in a review.

British Library Cataloguing in Publication Information Available

Library of Congress Cataloging-in-Publication Data Available
ISBN 9781475839388 (cloth: alk. paper) | ISBN 9781475839395 (pbk. : alk. paper) | ISBN 9781475839401 (electronic)

∞™ The paper used in this publication meets the minimum requirements of American National Standard for Information Sciences—Permanence of Paper for Printed Library Materials, ANSI/NISO Z39.48-1992.

Printed in the United States of America

We dedicate this book to all our students for their fierce desire to learn and their unflagging efforts to master this thing called college English.

Concetta Williams, EdD, and Lydia Magras, PhD

Contents

Foreword		ix
Abul Pitre		
Preface		xv
Introduction		xvii
1	Unpacking the History of African American Vernacular English	1
2	Teacher Perceptions of Their Students Who Speak AAVE	13
3	Closing the Gap: Connecting Students and Partnering AAVE and Collegiate Composition	27
4	Pedagogical Techniques for Teaching AAVE Speakers	49
5	What We Learned and What We Learnt	67
References		73
Index		79
About the Authors		85

Foreword

What I Learned and What I Learnt: Teaching English While Honoring Language and Culture at a Predominantly Black Institution is a very timely book considering the widespread discourse around educating Black students. It fits the Critical Black Pedagogy in Education Series by capturing the key elements of the series, which entails historical reflection to improve contemporary educational concerns.

This unique book explores language, literacy, and culture to offer a counternarrative to the deficit thinking that has caused educators to set low expectations for Black students. Exploring the rhetoric of "acting White," the authors detail the deeper meaning behind the phrase, arguing that contrary to the propaganda that Black people do not value education, the slogan "acting White" implies "looking down on me or treating me like I have been treated by White people."

Touching on subjects such as the Ebonics debate and teacher expectations, the book offers a pathway for educators to develop instructional materials that meet the needs of Black students. Moreover, the book includes historical data that is often overlooked in the education of Black students as it relates to language, literacy, and culture. It clearly demonstrates that the education of Black students should be studied in a historical context that explores the impact of slavery on language and literacy development. It surmises how the lived experiences of Blacks in the United States are deeply connected to the politics of education.

The education of Black people has always been a concern for America's ruling elite, causing them to spend millions of dollars crafting an educational agenda for Blacks in the United States. Historically, the state of Black education has been at the center of American life. When the first Blacks arrived in the Americas to be made slaves, a process of *miseducation* was systematized into the very fabric of American life. Newly arrived Blacks were dehumanized and forced through a process that has been described by a conspicuous slave owner named Willie Lynch as a "breaking process": "Hence the horse and the nigger must be broken; that is, break them from one form of mental life to another—keep the body and take the mind" (Hassan-El, 1999, p. 14). This horrendous process of breaking Blacks from one form of mental life to another included an elaborate educational system that was designed to kill the creative Black mind.

Elijah Muhammad called this a process that made Black people blind, deaf, and dumb—meaning the minds of Black people were taken from them. He proclaimed, "Back when our fathers were brought here and put into slavery 400 years ago, 300 [of] which they served as servitude slaves, they taught our people everything against themselves" (quoted in Pitre, 2015, p. 12). Woodson (2008) similarly decried, "Even schools for Negroes, then, are places where they must be convinced of their inferiority. The thought of inferiority of the Negro is drilled into him in almost every class he enters and almost in every book he studies" (p. 2).

Today, Black education seems to be at a crossroads. With the passing of the No Child Left Behind Act of 2001 and the U.S. Department of Education's Race to the Top, schools that serve a large majority of Black children have been under the scrutiny of politicians who vigilantly proclaim the need to improve schools while not realizing that these schools were never intended to educate or educe the divine powers within Black people. Watkins (2001) posits that after the Civil War, schools for Black people—particularly those in the South—were designed by wealthy philanthropists. These philanthropists designed "seventy-five years of education for blacks" (pp. 41–42). Seventy-five years from 1865 brings us to 1940. One has to consider the historical impact of seventy-five years of scripted education and its influence on the present state of Black education.

Presently, schools are still controlled by an elite ruling class that has the resources to shape educational policy (Spring, 2011). Woodson (2008) saw this as a problem in his day and argued, "The education of the Negroes, then, the most important thing in the uplift of Negroes, is almost entirely in the hands of those who have enslaved them and now segregate them" (p. 22). Here, Woodson cogently argues for historical understanding: "To point out merely the defects as they appear today will be of little benefit to the present and future generations. These things must be viewed in their historic setting. The conditions of today have been determined by what has taken place in the past" (p. 9). Watkins (2001) summarizes that "white architects of black education . . . carefully selected and sponsored knowledge, which contributed to obedience, subservience, and political docility" (p. 40). Historical knowledge is essential to understanding the plight of Black education.

A major historical point in Black education was the famous *Brown v. Board of Education of Topeka*, in which the U.S. Supreme Court ruled that segregation deprived Blacks of educational equality. Thus, schools were ordered to integrate with all deliberate speed. This historic ruling has continued to impact the education of Black children in myriad and complex ways.

To date, the landmark case of *Brown v. Board of Education of Topeka* has not lived up to its stated purpose. A significant number of schools in the twenty-first century continue to be segregated. Even more disheartening, schools that are supposedly desegregated may have tracking programs such as "gifted and talented" that attract White students and give schools the appearance of being integrated while being segregated within the school.

Spring (2006) calls this "second-generation segregation" and asserts: "Unlike segregation that existed by state laws in the South before the 1954 *Brown* decision, second-generation forms of segregation can occur in schools with balanced racial populations; for instance, all White students may be placed in one academic track and all African American or Hispanic students in another track" (p. 82). In this type of setting, White supremacy may become rooted in the subconscious minds of both Black and White students. Nieto and Bode (2012) highlight the internalized damage that tracking may have on students when they say students "may begin to believe that their placement in these groups is natural and a true reflection of whether they are 'smart,' 'average,' or 'dumb'" (p. 111).

According to Oakes and Lipton (2007), "African American and Latino students are assigned to low-track classes more often than White (and Asian) students, leading to two separate schools in one building—one [W]hite and one minority" (p. 308). Nieto and Bode (2012) argue the teaching strategy in segregated settings "leaves its mark on pedagogy as well. Students in the lowest levels are most likely to be subjected to rote memorization and static teaching methods" (p. 111).

These findings are consistent with Lipman's (1998) observation that "scholars have argued that desegregation policy has been framed by what is in the interest of [W]hites, has abstracted from excellence in education, and has been constructed as racial integration, thus avoiding the central problem of institutional racism" (p. 11). Darling-Hammond (2005) is not alone, then, in observing that "the school experiences of African American and other minority students in the United States continue to be substantially separate and unequal" (p. 202).

Clearly, the education of Black students must be addressed with a sense of urgency like never before. Lipman (1998) alludes to the crisis of Black education: "The overwhelming failure of schools to develop the talents and potentials of students of color is a national crisis" (p. 2). In just about every negative category in education, Black children are overrepresented. Again

Lipman (1998) suggests a crisis: "The character and depth of the crisis are only dimly depicted by low achievement scores and high rates of school failure and dropping out" (p. 2).

Under the guise of raising student achievement, the No Child Left Behind Act has instead contributed to the demise of educational equality for Black students. Darling-Hammond (2004) cites the negative impact of the law: "The Harvard Civil Rights Project, along with other advocacy groups, has warned that the law threatens to increase the growing dropout rate and pushout rates for students of color, ultimately reducing access to education for these students rather than enhancing it" (p. 4).

Asante (2005) summarizes the situation thus: "I cannot honestly say that I have ever found a school in the United States run by whites that adequately prepares black children to enter the world as sane human beings . . . an exploitative, capitalist system that enshrines plantation owners as saints and national heroes cannot possibly create sane black children" (p. 65). The education of Black students and the surrounding issues indeed make for a national crisis that must be put at the forefront of the African American agenda for liberation.

There is a need for a wide range of scholars, educators, and activists to speak to the issues of educating Black students. In the past, significant scholarly research has been conducted on the education of Black students; however, there does not seem to be a coherent theoretical approach to addressing Black education. Thus, there is a need to examine Black leaders, scholars, and activists, and their critique of the educational experiences of Black students. The Critical Black Pedagogy in Education Series is one such approach to addressing the educational challenges encountered by Black students. It is conceptually grounded in the educational philosophies of Elijah Muhammad, Carter G. Woodson, and others whose leadership and ideas could transform the educational experiences of Black students.

One can only imagine how schools would look if Muhammad, Woodson, Marcus Garvey, or other significant Black leaders were leading educational institutions. Through the study of critical Black educators, there is a possibility that an entirely new educational system could emerge. This new system should envision how Black leaders would transform schools within the context of our society's diversity. This would mean looking not only at historical Black leaders, but also at contemporary extensions of these leaders.

Karen Johnson (2014) describe the need for this perspective: "There is a need for researchers, educators, policy makers, etc. to comprehend the emancipatory teaching practices that African American teachers employed that in turn contributed to academic success of Black students as well as offered a vision for a more just society" (p. 99). Freire (2000) also lays a foundation for critical Black pedagogy in education by declaring that "it would be a contradiction in terms if the oppressors not only defended but actually implemented a liberating education" (p. 54).

What I Learned and What I Learnt: Teaching English While Honoring Language and Culture at a Predominantly Black Institution demonstrates how caring educators committed to social justice practices can transform the educational experiences of Black students. It positions historical knowledge to be a guide for improving the educational experiences of students from diverse backgrounds.

It is a welcome addition to the literature on Black education. Similar to Joyce King's (2005) *Black Education: A Transformative Research and Action Agenda for the New Century*, this book addresses research issues raised by the Commission on Research in Black Education (CORIBE). Like CORIBE, this book focuses on "using culture as an asset in the design of learning environments that are applicable to students' lives and that lead students toward more analytical and critical learning" (King, 2005, p. 353). The book is indeed provocative, compelling, and rich with information that will propel those concerned with equity, justice, and equality of education into a renewed activism.

Abul Pitre
Professor of Educational Leadership
Fayetteville State University

Preface

African Americans have viewed literacy as a key to upward mobility and freedom since before America's Reconstruction era. However, African Americans' academic achievement continues to be plagued by an ever-widening achievement gap when their literacy skills are measured by standardized assessments that do not consider or value their culture, their experiences, and their way of communicating, which may include using African American Vernacular English (AAVE).

Research and practical experiences suggest that African American students' achievement continues to be affected in this way at the postsecondary level. To help change this dynamic, this book is intended as a resource for those teaching speakers of AAVE at the postsecondary level. The book unpacks the history and system of AAVE, explores teachers' perceptions of the literacy skills of AAVE speakers and ideas about their role in teaching AAVE speakers, introduces ways to help speakers of AAVE make connections to mainstream English, and looks at pedagogical techniques.

Introduction

The chapters in this book reflect the range of experiences and methods used to help students who speak African American Vernacular English (AAVE) navigate spaces that privilege "marketplace" English. We lean on the research of Delpit (1995a, 1995b, 2002), Gee (1989a, 1989b, 1998, 2001, 2004, 2007), Gilyard (1999), Ladson-Billings (1994, 1995, 2002, 2005), and Smitherman (1977, 1994/2000, 1995, 2000) to anchor our discussions and definitions of discourse, literacy, and pedagogy.

We offer our experiences teaching speakers of AAVE as entry points into doing work that is motivated by our interest in propping open the door of opportunity and then helping students build a literacy toolkit once they have entered. We prop open this door so that students enter at their own free will, but we accept nothing but their maximum effort as we compassionately nudge them toward establishing a bilingual type of ability that allows them to hold true to their identities, and acquire tools that will help them in spaces where their identities are not celebrated.

Furthermore, we provide this text as an offering to other teachers struggling to help their students find a balance between the language that is closely linked to their community and culture, and the language they are expected to use for economic and social gain. Teachers who do not find a way to teach students to become fluent in the codes of power that govern mainstream contexts may actually ensure that the power differential or status quo continues to exist. As Delpit (1995a) describes, "When I speak, therefore, of the culture of power, I don't speak of how I wish things to be but of how they are. I further believe that to act as if power does not exist is to ensure that the power status quo remains the same" (p. 39).

In 1996, the Oakland Unified School District in Oakland, California, passed a resolution that would recognize "Ebonics" as the home language of its African American students. To that end, teachers would be required to address the language variations of African American students in the same way they would address the language variations of other bilingual students. With this resolution, the Oakland Board of Education (1996) also sought to address the disproportionate assessment scores of its African American students by pointing to how "such deficiencies will be remedied by application of a program featuring African Language Systems principles in instructing African American children both in their primary language and in English" (para. 7).

This resolution was met with debate from academics and the African American community, as some saw this as a means of "locking the gate" to the upward mobility that mastering mainstream English would provide. Others saw this as a step in the right direction as mainstream spaces finally acknowledged the language used by the African American community as a "first language" that is connected to culture and identity and that included a structure. There was hope that this resolution would reduce the intellectual assumptions that educational systems made about African American students based on language variations.

Although the Oakland resolution required teacher training in this area, there were limited academic resources to assist in doing this work. Also, the long-embedded perceptions held about Ebonics and its speakers were difficult to confront and undo. These assumptions have historical connections that are recycled throughout major governing systems that impact the day-to-day lives of African Americans. Many doubted if this resolution would be useful.

In 1998, the National Council of Teachers of English (NCTE) issued a position statement that addressed the negative view of the language variations used by African American students. NCTE's 1998 statement highlighted the ways media inject and reinforce negative portrayals of Ebonics, its speakers, and the debate surrounding it. The Conference on College Composition and Communication's Statement on Ebonics notes that "news media reports and commentaries regarding the recent Ebonics controversy have been, for the most part, incomplete, uninformed, and in some cases, purposefully distorted" (Conference on College Composition and Communication [CCCC], 1998, para. 2).

The statement defined and contextualized Ebonics as "a distinctive language system that many African American students use in daily conversation and in the performance of academic tasks" (CCCC, 1998, para. 3). The historical contextualization of Ebonics sought to demonstrate that Ebonics is a language system much like other languages, created for the same purpose as other languages, and that this language is useful for "daily conversation and in the performance of academic tasks," much like mainstream English. Simply put, Ebonics has the same purpose as any other language, and just because mainstream, White, middle-class society doesn't use it or understand it, doesn't make it bad or "less than."

The CCCC explicitly took on this issue and continues to do so through its Black Caucus. The 1998 statement issued by the CCCC was different from the Oakland resolution, as it (1) addressed the negative attitudes held about Ebonics and speakers of Ebonics as the obstacle to learning, instead of the language itself; (2) called for the training of professionals who are responsible for teaching students who speak Ebonics; and (3) called for additional research in the areas of teaching and Ebonics. The CCCC statement sought to confront the very idea that the perception of Ebonics has become a reality for its speakers. When the public considers Ebonics as a subpar form of communicating, they also extend that perception to its speakers and react to them with this perception rolling in the backdrop.

Twenty years later, the debate continues and the same historical perceptions about African American students hold firm. African American students continue to be stigmatized by educators, their experiences are not represented in academic materials, and their academic achievement continues to be documented as "behind" their White counterparts. Figure 0.1 reveals data from the 2017 ACT Condition of College and Career Readiness report. The figure shows the percentage of test takers who met ACT benchmarks (defined as being "college ready"). When we look specifically at the 2017 cohort of ACT-tested African American high school graduates compared to their White peers, we find steep differences in meeting benchmarks.

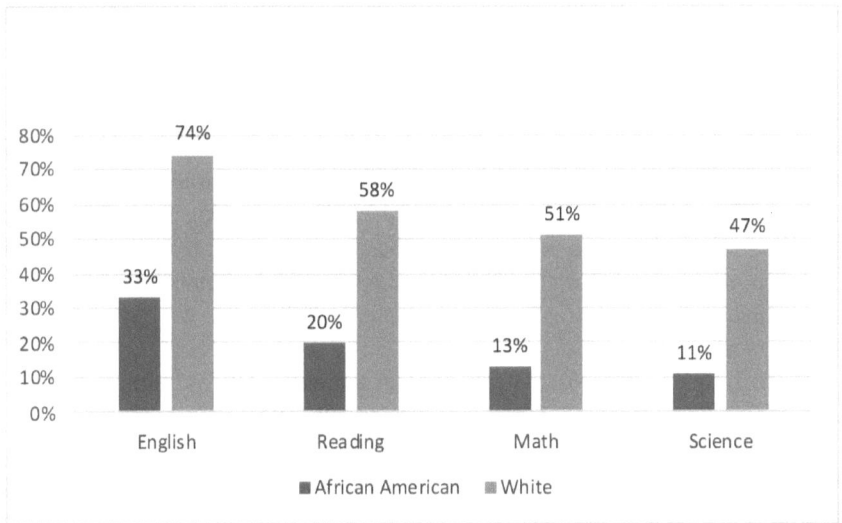

Figure 0.1. 2017 ACT tested high school graduate data.

The 2017 data reveal that the African American cohort not only lagged behind their White peers, but they lagged behind all testers. Whites were only second, and not by much, to Asian Americans who held the highest percentage of meeting benchmarks among all testers. Although English was the subject in which African American test takers did better, they were still 28 percent "behind" all students who tested and 41 percent behind their White peers.

In addition, African Americans were 27 percent "behind" in reading compared to all students who tested and 38 percent "behind" in reading compared to their White peers. This gap only widens when looking at the data for math and science. These data present a soft blow to a hard mountain. The data show that English is the subject in which African American students scored the highest on the ACT. This may lead some to question why African American students struggle in English courses when they get to college. The English section on the ACT is much different from college-level English courses. Therefore, the time spent preparing students to perform on the ACT and other standardized assessments do not actually prepare them to meet the expectations of college.

"English" is a combination of reading, writing, and communicating, which all work together to make up literacy skills. An assessment of college-readiness literacy skills would have to assess how these skills work in concert because that is the way they would be used at the postsecondary level. However, the data also suggest that there is a growing population of students who, regardless of their standardized assessment score, place into "developmental" or "remedial" English courses. Why? To resolve this tension, some postsecondary institutions are moving to using a standardized assessment score to place students into general education courses, which will eventually make it appear that fewer students need additional development to meet college literacy expectations.

What might result is an increase in the number of times a student repeats a course, if all other factors of classroom assessment remain intact. The intention of this text is not to speculate about these ideas or discuss the validity of standardized assessment; but because it has been accepted to some degree as a means of determining or predicting college success, these data at the very least must be considered, as they help define the ballpark in which the "game" is to be played.

With all this work to situate education as a means of upward mobility, how can African American students continue to "fall behind"? We continue to hear, in mostly White academic spaces, that the African American community equates academic success and fluency in Standard English (SE) as "acting and talking White." We hear this so much that we wanted to take time to address and attempt to contextualize these comments.

But why are we not having this conversation when low-income, poor Whites make similar statements ("You think you are better than me") to middle- or upper-class Whites? That is because *those* (poor, with limited education) White people are seen as the exception rather than the representatives of all of whiteness, whereas low-income life is seen as the prototypical "Black experience." True, in the African American community, people are sometimes accused of acting and talking White. However, this does not mean that African Americans do not value education, or that academic failure is a "Black" virtue.

The African American community values, appreciates, and celebrates education and understands the benefits that come from academic achievement. Contrary to popular belief, the African American community does not see education or academic success itself as "acting White." The phrases "acting White" or "talking White" are less about the attainment of education than the pretension that might accompany it.

It is this possibly pretentious behavior that sometimes comes with social and economic elevation that the Black community resists. It is our theory that when someone who has achieved academically is told to "Stop acting White," what is really being said is "You are looking down on me or treating me like I have been treated by White people who think I am less than them. Stop doing that because with all the education you have received, society still does not see you as equal to them, and don't forget they will remind you of it in the same way you are trying to show me that you are better than me."

In this instance, the person is seen to be "acting White" in that they are acting out a "White" identity of privilege for the purpose of being accepted by mainstream society. We also acknowledge the ways that mainstream society puts pressure on educated African Americans to separate themselves once they have achieved the "American dream."

In 1948, W. E. B. Du Bois addressed the idea of sacrifice and pretention in his "The Talented Tenth" remarks published in Sigma Pi Phi's *Boulé Journal*. Du Bois (1948) stated,

> Those Negroes who had long trained themselves for personal success and individual freedom, were coming to regard the disappearance of segregation as an end and not a means. They wanted to be Americans, and they did not care so much what kind of folk Americans were, as for the right to be one of them. They, not only, did not want to fight for a Negro culture, they even denied the possibility of any such animal, certainly its desirability even if it could be made to exist. (para. 14)

It is not an attack on the educational achievement, but an attack on any elitist tendency or attempt to assimilate to mainstream society by vehemently separating and downgrading others, especially those who may have sacrificed so that academic achievement could be possible for a few in the first place. Simply put, remember where you come from, and remember that to be educated and Black requires sacrifice and service to the forward movement of the race. Du Bois continues,

> My Talented Tenth must be more than talented, and work not simply as individuals. Its passport to leadership was not alone learning, but expert knowledge of modern economics as it affected American Negroes; and in addition to this and fundamental, would be its willingness to sacrifice and plan for such economic revolution in industry and just distribution of wealth, as would make the rise of our group possible. (para. 12)

We take up this discussion here because in chapter 2 we examine perceptions, and this is a common perception about the African American community—that African Americans do not value education. Our theory is meant to invite academics, especially those who train teachers, to reconsider this as a misperception.

So here we are as educators working from and within this space where we understand the "gaps" in access, opportunity, and perception. We understand the "gap" between African American and White students' academic achievement when measured by standardized assessments. We understand the "gap" in academic preparation often received by African American students. We also understand the "gap" in expectations held by teachers, at all levels, about their African American students' intellectual capacity and creativity. And that is where we find ourselves constantly standing, in the "gap" with our arms open, trying to keep the "gap" open as we fear it will close and crush our students.

CHAPTER SUMMARIES

Chapter 1 examines the rich history of AAVE. Before the discussion of Ebonics began formally in the twentieth century, there was recognition and debate about the existence of a Black language. This chapter explores the initial recordings of scholarly work in this area, including a discussion of theories of origin—the Anglican and the African based. We provide a detailed treatment of the legal cases—Ann Arbor, Michigan, and Oakland, California—that brought the subject to public attention.

In summary, the chapter explores the inextricable tethering of Black English to valuations of power assigned to language and used to suppress Blacks (and other people of color) in the United States. The insistence on the use of a particular form of the English language as spoken by the White, elite, Protestant founders of the country has worked its way into not just public education, but the very fabric of everyday life.

Chapter 2 explores the relationship between language and power in postsecondary settings. C. A. Williams (2014) conducted a study to uncover faculty's perceptions of their African American, first-time, full-time freshmen students' ability to interpret social cues in academic settings. That study revealed that participants saw their students' social literacy skills as being underdeveloped or not mature, which resulted in poor academic success. In this chapter, literacy is redefined in broader terms and social literacy is used to describe the ways that contexts shape the enactment of literacy beyond reading and writing.

Students' language use is something that teachers consider, in some way, in their classes and in their interactions with students. In addition, teachers consider this as they think about extending additional opportunities (internship or employment recommendation or consideration) to their students. Concetta also provides her experiences working with students on their own perceptions of AAVE when seen in print.

In chapter 3, Lydia compares and contrasts her teaching experiences to illustrate the central thesis of the text: that AAVE-centered understanding is critical to successful navigation of college-level composition courses by urban, first-generation college students. Recognizing her own transition as a scholar of literature to a composition faculty member, she highlights Dr. Carol Lee's (2007) cultural modeling approach as a method of incorporating AAVE into the classroom while also offering observations on the efficacy of cross-fertilizing Standard English (SE) with AAVE in instructional materials.

It was through her experience with speakers of English as a second language—trying to explain the finer points of SE like spatial relationships and using prepositions to describe such—that Lydia began to glimpse the inadequacy of traditional textbooks to address problems of English language mastery. And for the most part, her foreign students had another path to mastering English composition—classes that provided texts in both English *and* the language they spoke or practiced were offered.

And so began this budding idea that a different kind of textbook was needed to serve the needs of first-generation, urban college students (or English first language learners). This chapter specifies these needs, suggests some content for lesson plans, and begins the process for developing an applied pedagogy. It probes the morphology, phonology, and semantic features of both AAVE and SE. This approach privileges AAVE as a language of instruction for the mastery of SE. The chapter offers specific examples of SE instructional content and their AAVE counterparts.

Chapter 4 examines the work of Delpit (1995a, 1995b), Gee (1989a, 1989b, 1998, 2001), and Ladson-Billings (1994) as resources for developing instructional materials that take up the idea of social literacy skills and the ways they either open doors of opportunity for students, or close them. This chapter provides sample instructional materials that may serve as entry points into the larger discussion of spaces where marketplace or SE responses are expected. The activities are designed to help students make connections between AAVE and SE through schema building and activating activities.

OBJECTIVES

The major objective of this book is to extend the contemporary discourse on Ebonics/AAVE that began twenty years ago in California. Unlike the majority of books that have focused on Ebonics/AAVE in the K–12 educational settings, this book will discuss pedagogical approaches that are applicable to higher education classrooms. A major focus of the book is discussing classroom discourse for first-generation college students from urban backgrounds. This text takes a "we are all teachers of literacy" approach as it seeks to address the growing concern of postsecondary instructors in general.

It is common to hear postsecondary instructors say, "Our students can't read and write." This text enters the conversation in a candid way and provides examples of how students' literacy skills create a wedge between themselves and success, even when they earn a college degree. Many postsecondary instructors, of all disciplines, are aware of the challenges regarding language and literacy, but feel ill equipped to address it in their classrooms. This text provides practical approaches that can serve as a point of entry. Therefore, we hope the readership of this text will extend to both K–12 and postsecondary teachers within and outside colleges of education.

Teachers in K–12 settings can use this text as they take a practical approach to college readiness, and postsecondary instructors can use this text to build their instructional toolkit as they work to ready their students for careers. Furthermore, this text will also serve as a resource for preservice postsecondary instructors who seek to enter positions in settings where the mission is to provide access to underserved populations. This book can be used in courses such as multicultural education, language and literacy, teaching reading through literature, and English as a second language.

AUTHORS' PERSPECTIVES

We arrived at this book after presenting a roundtable discussion, "Literacy in the Lives of African Americans," at a meeting of the Association for the Study of African American Life and History (ASALH) conference. The conference became the impetus for developing a resource that could help practitioners fine-tune their approach to teaching students who, unlike SE language learners, speak English as a first language but speak a dialect of English that is rooted in their (non–White middle class) culture and community. Here, we provide our perspectives and approaches to the writing of this book.

Concetta's Perspective

As a former director of a first-year writing program, the doorway to my office was often the gathering spot for faculty members who either wanted to discuss an interesting sentence in a piece of student writing or wanted to discuss the many ways that school systems had underprepared students to meet the literacy expectations of higher education contexts. Many of these office doorway dwellers were from outside the English department, and their initiation of the discussions about writing could be interpreted as a call for assistance. Just as they were trying to interpret what their students were trying to say, they were standing in my doorway asking me to interpret what *they* were trying to say.

In the end, all conversations translated into one basic word: "Help!" The implicit message embedded in these discussions was not only dissatisfaction with the tangible literacy-driven artifacts that students provided, but disappointment with the intangible literacy-driven artifacts students left them with after an actual interaction. After much thought and probing, it seemed as though the faculty members in my doorway were communicating concern about their students' inability to demonstrate literacy skills based on the context. Implicit in their discussions about their students were concerns about helping students develop in this area without sending a message that devalued the language they spoke. They needed and wanted direction in this area.

Theory suggests that language, community, culture, and mainstream expectations may pose a conflict (Delpit, 2002; Gee, 1998, 2001; Ladson-Billings, 1994; Smitherman, 1977, 1994/2000, 1995, 2000) between students and instructors. Students bring a variety of experiences that teacher education encourages us to see as assets. In the case of diverse educational settings where students' experiences may not be aligned to middle-class or mainstream values, those assets turn into hurdles. Gee (2001) states that language is used as a means of determining whether one is a member of a certain discourse community, or an imposter. In this instance, the doorway dwellers were saying that they were teaching a bunch of imposters.

As teachers in diverse settings, we understand all too well the implicit implications for demonstrating one's membership through discourse. We understand that our students traverse rough terrain as they enter our classrooms from unique communities. They use discourse to make an explicit announcement about their membership in academic discourse communities in an implicit way. For teachers, we then have to do the work of massaging these discourse habits so that our students do not shut doors before they are ever opened. We have to move our conversations out of doorways with colleagues and into our classrooms.

Furthermore, faculty of color must remember the lessons we learned and those we learnt as we traveled similar paths as our students. I often move between AAVE and SE in my classroom to demonstrate how this is purposefully done. We must replace judgment with compassion and action. For that, we need the resources.

Lydia's Perspective

Although I consider myself fluent in Black English, it was Zora Neale Hurston who focused my scholarly attention to this thing called Black language, the phenomenon also known as AAVE. Her 1934 essay, "The Characteristics of Negro Expression," served as a second stepping-off point for my research into AAVE.

As a teacher of introductory composition at the collegiate level, my teaching practicums trained me to address the writing needs of the well-educated (translation: products of well-funded local school systems). The finer points of language arts—specifically the logic behind the construction of sentences—were not the focus. Instead, my students were primarily tutored in coming up with ideas. It was through my experience with speakers of English as a second language that I began to glimpse the inadequacy of traditional textbooks to address problems of English language mastery.

But it was my experiences in an urban college, attended by mostly adult, Black, first-generation college students, that solidified my research interests. How to transliterate the assigned rhetoric texts into language that my students, fluent speakers of AAVE, could understand became a daily challenge. "Where are the relevant texts that answer this question?" became my prayerful plea. My chapters represent an attempt to frame a response.

Chapter 1

Unpacking the History of African American Vernacular English

In 1994, noted Black linguist Geneva Smitherman proffered a definition of Black English as "a set of communication patterns and practices resulting from Africans' acquisition, appropriation, and/or transformation of a foreign tongue during the African Holocaust" (Smitherman, 1994/2000, p. 19). The determination of the genesis of Black English has consumed the research activities of linguists for quite some time. The two prevailing theories—whether Black English is a direct derivative of African dialects or whether it was born from the experience of Africans dropped off in the Caribbean—continues to be debated.

This latter theory is perhaps more relevant to the modern-day world of word creation—or, as Zora Neale Hurston might describe it, the "will to adorn" (Hurston 1934/1994, p. 79) that results in unique and highly descriptive characterizations of the environment as experienced by the Black man and woman in the United States. Consider the additions of *fleek* and *twerk* to the American English lexicon. Geneva Smitherman summarizes the genesis of Black English thusly: "African American language represents a dual heritage" (1994/2000, p. 5) in a state of double consciousness. Vestiges of African language (lexicon and grammar) combine with aspects of the English spoken by European Americans.

As we move through a review of the history of Black English in the United States, we must conduct that review through a prism that refracts the truth that language—any language—is used to enforce ideological goals. Linguist and political scientist Noam Chomsky (1988/2004) often writes about such a prism and the ideological uses of language, offering reasons why Black English (or African American Vernacular English [AAVE]) is so disrespected—a reality at the heart of all research about the dialect:

> Language has often proved to be a source of tension and misunderstanding [rather] than [one] of unity and universal love ... language differentiation is also a source of cultural variety and the excitement that results from it ... divisiveness ... is merely a special case of the conflict caused by chauvinism, group identification, or cultural difference. (p. 127)

We will apply these tenets of language analysis in the following historical review of the genesis of Black English in America. There are two prevailing schools of thought. The model based on an evolution from African-based traditions and the "linguistic continuum throughout the African diaspora" (Smitherman, 2000) is the least likely to promote the kind of divisiveness that Chomsky identifies. The second, or Anglican, theory argues that everything African was eradicated during the hardships of the middle passage and the aftermath of slavery, a point of view that, according to Smitherman (2000), remained unchallenged in mainstream linguistics until the 1960s. The supporters of this claim can be arguably categorized as dissing both the validity and relevance of Black English.

The African genesis theory is supported by Mufweme (2000), who argues definitively that "African languages influenced Africans in North America to re-articulate and integrate English features ... differently from [those] of [their] European counterparts" (p. 234). His thesis is supported by examples from linguistic considerations, specifically grammatical forms of Black English. In fact, Mufweme asserts that Africans brought to North America actually created a new dialectical system, one that is the direct ancestor to modern-day Black English and one that "restructured," "re-articulated," and "reorganized ... from extant systems" (2000, p. 234).

In other words, from the moment of their arrival on the shores of North America, Africans strove to incorporate the vestiges of what they knew of their native languages; remnants of that were carefully, secretly, and lovingly cherished. Mufweme bases his conclusions on comparative studies of slave narratives and a re-interpretation of the founder principle from the science of genetics. As he points out, over time, the number of African slaves born in the United States began to outnumber those who were forced to immigrate. And so, "the newcomers sought to adapt to the local norms, rather than impose their own" (Mufweme, 2000, p. 240).

This divergence led to Africanisms becoming embedded in the restructured English of the earliest arrivals and reinforced by those transported later. Rickford and Rickford (2000), who would appear to subscribe to the reality of the African roots of Black English, also identified detractors of this school of thought. John McWhorter, who specializes in the formation of creole languages, emphatically states that Black English is "not traceable to West

Africa" (Rickford & Rickford, 2000, p. 152) and, by default, not traceable to Africa at all.

Likewise, Ernie Smith, who is credited as a cocreator of the word Ebonics in 1973, calls Black English an "oxymoron because [it] doesn't follow English grammar rules" (Rickford & Rickford, 2000, p. 152). As we will see later, there are others who have identified the linguistic convergences between Black English and Standard English (SE), specifically as relates their constructions of grammar rules.

Rickford and Rickford (2000, p. 175) continue: "As of this writing, there is still a division between those who attribute Ebonics origin to Africa and those who don't." And yet Smitherman (2000) avers firmly that none of the research fully accounts "for the historical development of [Black English]" (p. 32), citing the work of Dillard (1972) and Stewart (1972) as evidence that Black English is not simply a dialect of English.

J. L. Dillard (1972) concurs: "American linguistics has failed to provide accurate information about Black English because of the myopic nature of the historical work on American English" (p. 3). It can be argued that the nature of such historical work is myopic for several reasons, not the least of which is a serious consideration of the influence of the languages of voluntary immigrants to the United States, to say nothing of the language contributions to SE made by the original inhabitants of the land—the Native Americans.

Another perspective is the so-called divergence hypothesis that was developed by Labov and Harris (1986) to explain linguistic phenomena that occurred during the 1915 Great Migration of Blacks away from the Deep South. They point out the differences in Black and White vernaculars, in particular aspects of phonology (related to the sound of a word) that were not shared. The authors attributed such differences to an effect of segregation. People speak like those with whom they have the most and closest contact. Although Blacks and Whites had contact in the rigidly segregated South, Blacks were not as free to speak when in the presence of Whites—a holdover from the unspoken rules of slavery.

Baugh (2000) marks an early entry point for the study of Black English, in the fifteenth century. His discussion introduces the idea that American English has been heavily influenced by speakers of other languages. According to Baugh, Columbus did not come into contact with Native American languages, but Dillard (1972) notes that there was a definite Portuguese impact on the lexicon of American English. Dillard specifically identifies Pedro Alonzo Niño, who traveled with Columbus to the New World. For example, the word *pickaninny*, which came to be applied to young African slaves in America and, according to Dillard, is of Portuguese derivation, can be traced directly back to Niño. Its presence in the standard English vocabulary supports

Baugh's (2000) thesis that Africanized English can be documented as early as the fifteenth century.

In considering the expansion of the slave trade, Baugh's contention that American English is influenced by speakers of other languages gives birth to speculation about how the enslaved learned to speak the language of their slave masters. A Dutch frigate brought twenty Africans to Virginia in 1620 (Mufweme, 2000), and while they were in fact indentured servants and not slaves (a distinction of little merit), the idea arose that these Africans spoke an English that simply mimicked what they heard.

Although there are no studies of the language question from that period, Smitherman (2000) points out that we cannot overlook that period as one of incubation for Black English. In the second half of the seventeenth century, Africans began to be dropped off in the Caribbean, which gave rise to another idea about the character of the English acquired by slaves: the inclusion of linguistic markers present in places like St. Kitts and Barbados, where the population of slaves grew more due to births than due to importation.

Again, the newer slaves began to acquire language as it was spoken by those who had been on site longer, rather than directly imitating their White slave masters. Smitherman (2000) makes it clear that Black English did not solely originate in British English, nor in other White immigrant dialects from the seventeenth century.

While the eighteenth century saw greater numbers of Africans kidnapped into slavery, these Africans were also learning English from other Blacks. As the internal slave trade developed through movement from north to south and, to some extent, west, Black English speech acts became an identity marker; "a [demonstrated] aversion to kinship with whites and their brutality" (Rickford & Rickford, 2000, p. 138)—a fact that has implications for contemporary acquisition of Black English.

Of course, there was certainly the development of a type of pidgin English, which Dillard (1972) describes as a language that has no native speaker. As Africans were dropped off in the Caribbean isles—some say to be tamed before shipment to America, although there was certainly work to be done processing the locally grown sugar cane—their presence resulted in interaction between the Africans and Caribe Indians. Their Africanized Pidgin English evolved into plantation creole, "a language that was pidgin at an earlier historical stage, but that [becomes] the only [or principal] language of a speech community" (Dillard, 1972, p. 300). Mufweme (2000, p. 245) argues that "socio-economic history suggests that the influence of Caribbean creoles on the development of [Black] English seems to have been exaggerated."

THE INFLUENCE OF EMANCIPATION, MIGRATION, AND JIM CROW

The first representations of slave speech in literature occurred in the eighteenth century (Smitherman, 2000). But more importantly, as Chomsky (1988/2004) notes, the eighteenth-century speech succeeded in going beyond what has been called the first emancipation phase of history, to the one that made serfs out of slaves, and then to the phase that made wage earners out of serfs. This transition from serfdom to wage earner was facilitated by the accelerated movement of Blacks, and would have a lasting effect on the transmission and acquisition of Black English.

The 1879 exodus of 20,000 Blacks migrating to Kansas helped to consolidate speech patterns across the United States (Mufweme, 2000). The Great Migration during the first quarter of the twentieth century, when 20 million Africans left the south, according to Mufweme, provided the first socioeconomic ecology for linguistic divergence. In spite of some nineteenth-century regional differences or varieties of Black English, this stabilization was reinforced well into the twentieth century.

If the 1879 exodus was the first major migration of Black Americans, a second wave followed the Emancipation Proclamation. This second wave featured its own linguistic import: increased exposure to so-called Standard English, resulting from increased access to education, an exposure lessened by the forced segregation mandated during Reconstruction. The rise of Jim Crow laws fostered a renewed and particularly virulent return to the Anglican philosophy about Black English.

James Harrison's *Negro English*, published in 1884, actively promoted "African-ness as pathological" (Rickford & Rickford, 2000, p. 144). In addition, it is worth a reminder that H. L. Mencken's *The American Language* (1919/1937) contained subtle yet insidious suggestions regarding the truth of a Black [language] inadequacy. And yet, Black English survived as a "seething oppositional identity" (Rickford & Rickford, 2000, p. 144) with force and power.

Dillard (1972) proposes that "Black English is a human language and it ... has a history as [does] any other language" (p. 34). John Baugh (2000) completes the argument by noting that "all human languages and dialects are equal in the eyes of science, even if they are not considered equal in the eyes of the law," but rather colored with "linguistic shame ... trauma ... and chauvinism" (p. 115).

DEFINING BLACK ENGLISH

Early attempts to define Black English often described it as a "veneer" contrived for the White boss man (Dillard, 1972, p. 8). An example is H. L. Mencken's assessment of the early American slave narratives in that he claims weren't produced until the time of the Civil War (Dillard, 1972, p. 12) and may have in fact been written by White people. A definitive 1924 study, "The English of the Negro" by George Philip Krapp, asserts that Black English is an "imperfect and inadequate imitation of European American . . . baby talk between master and slave" (quoted in Smitherman,1994/2000, p. 74).

The emergence of the deviant model descriptor of Black English viewed the variety, and "Black culture generally, as deficient and pathological" (Smitherman, 2000, p. 71). Smitherman continues: "In the years just before the Civil War (roughly the 1840s and 1850s), scientific theories of racial superiority located social and behavioral differences between members of the human species in genetic factors" (p. 71). This point of view, which is enjoying a fierce resurgence today, set the stage for separation of the races and the establishment of Jim Crow policies. Contemporary scholars have also weighed in on this topic.

Quoting Smitherman, Lee (2007) offers the following context: "[it] is widely noted that the most studied and demonized dialect of American English" (p. 80) is Black English. The default assumption, Lee continues, is that "ways of using language deemed vernacular hold no hands with the demand of reasoning" (p. 80). And yet Krapp surmises that "an important factor in the evolution of languages and dialects is an accurate evolution of the languages and dialects of the present" (quoted in Dillard, 1972, p. 18). Additional voices in support of the evolving African American Vernacular English began to appear. According to Smitherman, both W. E. B. Du Bois and Carter G. Woodson asserted that "African American cultural distinctions [in language] resulted from retentions and adaptations of African culture to new circumstances and conditions" (Smitherman, 2000, p. 33). And of course, 1934 saw the publication of Zora Neale Hurston's analysis of Black language in her article, "The Characteristics of Negro Expression," which further solidified this connection, citing the Negro's [sic] Africanisms and creativity in what can be considered a foundational text on Black English.

Hurston's essay introduces us to a structural analysis of Black English, referring as she does to the reason for the use of unusual descriptors, metaphors, and the like. Melville J. Herskovits's *Myth of the Negro Past* (1941) added fuel to the fire under the Africana theory of origin. His text quoted from an unpublished manuscript by Lorenzo Dow Turner, a scholar of some significance in the field of African linguistics. Herskovits considered

Turner's work as proof that "Blacks did indeed have a past—[an] African cultural and linguistic heritage—and that past continued to survive in the present" (quoted in Smitherman, 2000, p. 76).

The twentieth century also saw a rebirth of interest in the naming of Black people. Smitherman (2000) notes that the 1920s saw a massive campaign to capitalize Negro, which was the label of choice for the time. This move was only the latest in a series: African, Colored, Negro, and continuing on to Black and African/Afro-American.

LINGUISTICS AND BLACK ENGLISH

Following a hiatus of significant research on the subject during the 1940s and 1950s, a period that witnessed the emergence of a decidedly more subtle form of racist ideology (in general and around Black language in particular), a virtual explosion burst onto the scene in the 1960s and 1970s. In a nod to prevailing research trends around environment and social conditioning, coupled with the impact of the Black Power movement, American linguists initiated studies of Black English's impact on language.

They began with attempts to name it: Negro Non-Standard, Black English Vernacular (BEV), and African American Vernacular English (AAVE); according to Rickford and Rickford (2000), these were all coined by White linguists such as J. L. Dillard, William Labov, and William Stewart. Rickford and Rickford (2000) are fond of the term "spoken soul," but Baugh (2000) has surmised that the term Black English is far more common.

Structural analysis of linguistic features continued to dominate the conversation. Drilling down into this study of Black English does in fact demonstrate the features that define a language: morphology (word forms), phonology (word sounds), a lexicon or vocabulary, contextual semantic meanings, and even grammar. It even fits the format that Chomsky (1988/2004) offers as a matrix for all languages. Chomskyan linguistics names "a system of rules and principles, finite in size that assign representations of sound and meaning to an infinite array of sentences . . . that are structure dependent and apply to abstract structures imposed on a linguistic signal by the mind, and not by the signal itself" (Chomsky, 1988/2004, p. 350).

What is determined by the analysis of sentences is the breakdown of these structures into *surface* and *deep* (Chomsky's terms). *Deep structure* refers to the cognition that forms the context for the linguistic signal or speech act or sentence. *Surface structure* refers to the analysis of whether the speech act or sentence complies with grammar rules and principles. AAVE has often taken a beating because of its apparent disregard for rules and principles of grammar, but a study of the grammar of AAVE reveals this hypothesis to be untrue. For as Smitherman (2000) reminds us, AAVE "is a set of communication patterns and practices resulting from Africans' appropriation and transformation of the [rules and principles] of a foreign tongue" (p. 19). An abridged focus on verbs, intentional markers, and prepositions will serve to illustrate the point.

In the mid-twentieth century, Rickford and Rickford (2000) pointed out distinct differences between Black English and Standard English: the use of *be* to indicate a never-changing duration or habitual state: *I be walking*, meaning *I am walking now and I will continue to walk*. In another variation of AAVE's use of the copula, the helping verb is omitted: *He tall*. Smitherman (2000) attributes such forms of omission to the non-obligatory nature of usage in West African languages and, to some extent, creole languages.

Another variation finds the addition of the verb *been* in the position of a helping verb: *They done been sitting there a whole hour* (Smitherman, 2000). The additional verb is used to emphasize a completed action. The use of *here go/there go* is another example: *There go my Momma in the front row* (Smitherman, 2000), again as an emphasizing accent when no motion is occurring. The mother is simply sitting in her seat in the front row. There is also the ever-present *fitna* or *finna* to communicate the immediate future: *I'm finna go to the store*, meaning *I am preparing to go to the store*.

These are all examples of how Black English verb usage privileges *aspect*—how an action extends over time—over verb tense. These examples also directly connect to Hurston's (1934/1994) identification of the Black man's will to adorn his statements—to add or coin words for emphasis and style. Or take Asante's linguistic analysis, as reported by Rickford and Rickford (2000), of serial verbs like *I hear tell*. Such constructions connect to Hurston's revelation that the Black man thinks in pictures, and consequently his speech reflects his vision.

Conversely, sometimes the speech act is one of camouflage: *She was indignant when she began speaking to me* becomes *She come telling me* (Smitherman, 2000). The final examples, also provided by Smitherman (2000), note AAVE's usage of *ain but* and *don't but* for limited negation: *She ain nothing but a kid. Don't but two people know*. A commonly heard non-profane expletive or filler in the speech of AAVE is the existential *it*: *Is it anybody home?* Again, emphasis and adornment of the thought seem to be key.

There are two points to be made about these observances. First, the use of morpheme markers to indicate the future tense (e.g., *gon/gonna*) represents a direct borrowing by Black English from other languages (Mufweme, 2000). Black English also incorporates distinctly African compound words like *tote*, *okay*, *goober*, and *cut-eye* (Rickford & Rickford, 2000). Second, a comparative analysis of Black English with regional vernaculars leads to the work of

Robert Williams, who defines Black English in accordance with two major dimensions in language: lexicon and morphology.

In 1973, Williams convened a conference titled "Cognitive and Language Development in the Black Child." The conference drew on many of the themes later articulated in Williams's 1975 text, *Ebonics: The True Language of Black Folks*. Williams, a "critic and resistor to standardized tests and their inherent cultural biases," coined the word *Ebonics* as a blend of the words *ebony* and *phonetics* and as a way of "defining our own language" (Baugh, 2000, p. 216).

Ebonics may be defined as the linguistic and paralinguistic features that on a concentric continuum represent the communicative competence of West African, Caribbean, and North American slave descendants of African origin. It includes the grammar, various idioms, patois, argots, idiolects, and social dialects of Black people (R. Williams, 1975). In this way Williams both revived and rebirthed the discussion begun by Hurston. The discussion of naming was revisited in 1988 by Dr. Ramona Edelin, who was the first to propose "African American English" as the descriptor (Smitherman, 2000).

The influence of Williams's work was seen in the case of the Ann Arbor Decision of 1979. In 1974, the federal government of the United States promulgated the Equal Education Opportunity Act (EEOA), a federal law that prohibited discrimination against faculty, staff, and students, including racial segregation of students, and required school districts to take action to overcome barriers to students' equal participation.

Three years later, in 1977, a group of parents of Black students at the Martin Luther King Jr. Elementary School sued the Ann Arbor School Board based on the EEOA. While enrollment at the school was predominantly White and upper class, the student population was 13 percent urban Black. Concerned about the reading achievement levels of their children (or more accurately, the lack of achievement), the Black parents charged school officials with improperly placing these students in learning disability and speech pathology classrooms (Smitherman, 2000).

The defense countered that the placements were appropriate, saying that "perhaps the children were uneducable" (quoted in Smitherman, 2000, p. 113). Discovery in the case revealed that evaluations of the children in question failed to uncover any inherent limitation in the children's cognitive or language capacities. In the judgment of the professional consultants brought in to review the case, the "children were normal, intelligent kids who could learn if properly taught" (Smitherman, 2000, p. 113).

If properly taught would be the linchpin of the case and is, in fact, an underlying claim in the thesis of this text. In 1979, Judge Charles W. Joiner ruled that "on the basis of failing to overcome language barriers, the Ann Arbor School District had violated the children's right to equal educational opportunity" (Smitherman, 2000, p. 132). By ruling in this way, Joiner indicated that the use of Black English by students was not the problem; it was *the school's response* to this language difference that was at issue.

This was a breakthrough moment for Black students, even though the ruling failed on other counts. "All claims relative to economic, social, and cultural factors were dismissed" (Smitherman, 2000, pp. 133–34), meaning the U.S. Constitution can provide protection on the basis of being Black, but "not on the basis of being poor" (p. 134).

What a precedent this ruling set. Its implications can be seen, if one looks closely, in the current state of public education in U.S. urban centers. Poor children are routinely miseducated, if not through the burgeoning charter school movement, certainly through the articulated policies of the current U.S. Secretary of Education, Betsy DeVos.

Geneva Smitherman, who was an expert witness and plaintiff on the Ann Arbor case, concludes her 1981 article on the proceedings by identifying a critical strategy for tackling Black English in the classroom: "[We cannot] specify educational goals for Blacks apart from considerations about the structure of [White] American society" (2000, p. 57). The power dynamics demand such an approach. Lee (2007) concurs: "What would have been the trajectory of achievement [of the Ann Arbor students] had [they] experienced instruction from elementary school forward and across subject matter . . . that was designed to scaffold their prior knowledge and community based experiences in ways that mapped strategically onto the demands of the [curriculum]" (p. 91).

What indeed? Dillard (1972) framed the position in this way: "A judgement in favor of a child's speech ability in preference to another's is very likely a value judgement expressing an attitude that favors one child's culture over that of the other" (p. 269). This bias, as Dillard terms it, is at the crux of the history of Black English in the United States. And Chomsky (1988/2004) claps back at the custodians of history whose privilege and authority are used to devalue AAVE, which they demonize as a threat to their control of access to free inquiry.

The debate over the nature of Black English was revived again in 1996 when the Oakland Unified School District's board issued a resolution recognizing Black English as a second language. The intent of the resolution was to grant speakers of Black English the same sort of educational support that other non-SE speakers received from the school system. Faced with failing national test scores and a disproportionate level of suspensions and truancies, the framers of the resolution were concerned with issues of education, not linguistics (Rickford & Rickford, 2000).

The dispute lay in *how* this goal was to be achieved (Rickford & Rickford, 2000). A separation between the linguistic deconstruction of English and its application in education seemed to be the answer. The Oakland Board of Education's philosophy, as its subsequent resolution reflected, became to "teach mainstream English by contrasting it with the home language [of the students] (Rickford & Rickford, 2000, p. 175). Carving out such a distinction was problematic, and remains so to this day.

The Black community itself was torn over the issue. Vociferous opposition from the Reverend Jesse Jackson (though he later reversed his stance) and a robust debate in the news media, barbershops, and churches in the Black community were combined with negative reactions to the word Ebonics among Black conservatives. The opposition was widely seen as tied to the aspirations for deeper integration that Dillard identified as early as 1972. Baugh (2000, p. 112) described the reaction as a "nearly universal linguistic shame" regarding Black English. He also noted that the problem was not so much the word Ebonics itself, and quoted a W. E. B. Du Bois statement from 1928: "If a thing is despised either because of ignorance or because it is despicable, you will not change matters by changing its name" (Baugh, 2000, p. 1).

The Ebonics movement failed because of competing definitions of terms, general public outrage, and a failure to promote linguistic tolerance (Baugh, 2000). However, some progress was made. The Oakland resolution was accepted into California curriculum, and although it was never fully implemented in elementary and secondary schools, materials were created that presented content in contexts that were culturally relevant to Black (and Brown) students. Unfortunately, the same could not be said for texts in wide usage on college and university campuses. In the years since the Oakland resolution, interest in Black English as a second language in educational pedagogy waned, and in the revised set of recommendations released by Oakland in May 1997, all references to Ebonics were erased (Rickford & Rickford, 2000).

Chapter 2

Teacher Perceptions of Their Students Who Speak AAVE

> Every time a student sits down to write for us, he has to invent the university for the occasion.... The student has to learn to speak our language, to speak as we do, to try on the peculiar ways of knowing, selecting, evaluating, reporting, concluding, and arguing that define the discourse of our community. (Bartholomae, 1986, p. 4)

This chapter addresses students' use of AAVE in academic contexts, and the concept of social literacy. *Social literacy* refers to literacy-related skills (reading and communicating) that people use during their transactions with either the spoken word or context (C. A. Williams, 2014). Learning does not occur in isolation of experience, but is influenced by social contexts (Rosenblatt, 1994). The human being is seen as part of a larger context or "nature" who makes sense of new situations by applying it to previous exposure (Rosenblatt, 1994; Stanovich, 2004).

Bartholomae's words in the epigraph remind teachers that their students are in a place of transition when they enter their classrooms. They are often trying to "invent" a space for which they have little schema to aid in their version or invention. Students who have been socialized outside of what are considered mainstream environments—those closely aligned with White middle-class ways of knowing—may find that their efforts, no matter how earnest, result in a version of the university that is not closely enough aligned to its expectations to lead to academic or social success.

In particular, students' invention of the university, in terms of enacting its discourse, is one of the first places where students are challenged and faculty develop a perception of students. Here, we focus the discussion on speakers of AAVE and teachers' perceptions of them. These students are in a unique position because they speak English as a first language, but they primarily speak what is considered a dialect of the English language—one that is closely aligned to their own culture and community, but distant from what is considered mainstream. This makes the challenge of providing instruction unique as well.

RESOLUTIONS AND STATEMENTS REGARDING AAVE AND INSTRUCTION

At the time of the 1996 Oakland Unified School District's Ebonics resolution, leaders and scholars in the African American community and other primary speakers of AAVE had a difficult time reaching a unified position on AAVE, its status as a language, and its place in academic instruction. Some would argue that this is the result of decades of discrimination or a "sense of always looking at one's self through the eyes of others, of measuring one's soul by the tape of a world that looks on in amused contempt and pity" (Du Bois, 1903/1994, p. 7).

Starting in 1974 and continuing in revised forms ever since, the National Council of Teachers of English (NCTE) issued a statement titled "Students' Right to Their Own Language." This statement reminded teachers that AAVE is not an obstacle for learning; rather, it is the negative attitudes held about AAVE and its speakers that serve as the obstacle to student success. To an extent, these resolutions turned a mirror on teachers and encouraged us to consider how *our* attitudes and perceptions impact our students. Furthermore, there was a call for teacher training in these areas.

Many teacher preparation programs and graduate programs have yet to streamline a teaching approach for this population of learners. Furthermore, postsecondary faculty are seldom required to attain a teaching license; therefore, they tend to be content experts, but may have limited formal or academic preparation in pedagogy. Scholars such as Lisa Delpit, Geneva Smitherman, and Keith Gilyard have provided a framework for teaching and learning in contexts greatly populated with AAVE speakers.

These contexts are not limited to urban communities, as people would like to believe. According to Hussar and Bailey (2013), college enrollment of African American students is expected to increase by 26 percent by 2022. Thus, our discussion not only applies to teaching spaces identified as historically Black, predominantly Black, or minority serving, but extends to predominantly White academic spaces. However, it is these historically and predominantly Black spaces, and the ways even those faculty have a difficult time helping students navigate various discourse communities, that we examine here.

What we have learned from our colleagues in K–12 settings is that we have a troop of teachers entering and currently in the profession who are unprepared to talk about race on deep and meaningful levels and unprepared to address the nuanced ways that students' experiences shape how they show up in our classrooms and how they function in academic settings (Koss & Williams, 2018). For too long we have trained teachers to make statements such as "I don't see color; all I see are students." Research tells us that is not true. We see color, we hear voice, and we judge. It is our responsibility to acknowledge and check that predisposition so that it does not seep into our classrooms and taint our perceptions and influence our choices as teachers.

AAVE IN ACADEMIC SETTINGS

We hear the melodic tones of AAVE in the hallways through conversations between students, between faculty and, at times, between faculty and students. These conversations utilizing AAVE are also in our classrooms. To that end, we can either "shut it down" immediately and establish the classroom as a formal space where only academic language (SE) is expected with no clarification or discussion, or we can be honest with our students about how they may be perceived as members of the academic discourse community based on the language they use. Some teachers may even use this to determine if these students *should* be a part of the academic community in the first place.

If one accepts that AAVE is a fully developed language, as linguistic study has proved it is, then we can move from a stance of eradication to one of *culturally sustaining pedagogy* (CSP) to help students find ways to maintain the language they use, which is tied to their culture and identity, while also establishing a practice for using SE, which is privileged in academic contexts (Paris, 2012). CSP seeks to help students maintain their cultural identity and all artifacts associated with it while attaining proficiency in mainstream discourse. Specifically, "CSP seeks to perpetuate and foster—to sustain—linguistic, literate, and cultural pluralism as part of the democratic project of schooling and as a needed response to demographic and social change" (Paris & Alim, 2014).

Recent reports tell us that the way teachers *perceive* their students has an impact on how discipline—specifically exclusionary—is distributed in schools, and how teachers determine which students' experiences are valued (see Gershenson, Hart, Lindsay, & Papageorge, 2017; Gilliam, Maupin, Reyes, Accavitti, & Shic, 2016). Although these reports focus on K–12 settings, we know that the impact of teachers' perceptions about their students do not end at that point. Students must negotiate and, to an extent, manage these often unknown perceptions throughout their time in college.

Much of this discussion will examine the results of C. A. Williams's (2014) study that examined university faculty's perceptions of first-year African American students' ability to navigate academic spaces. This study took place at a Midwestern, predominantly Black four-year university. Findings from this study revealed that participants tended to generalize about students and see students as unprepared to meet the challenges of higher education for a variety of reasons. Chief among their reasons was a belief that the way students communicated reinforced this perception, and when asked, teachers acknowledged that most of their students used AAVE to communicate both verbally and in writing. There was a perception that students were capable of meeting academic expectations, but did not want to rise to the occasion.

Gee (2007) tells us that language is used to either establish one's membership in a particular context or announce that one is not a member. In this case, teachers had determined that their students were not members of the legitimate academic community and questioned if they ever would be. As we examine research that presents teachers' reported perceptions of students who speak AAVE in the classroom and how they respond to those students, we aim to bring forth these perceptions and the ways they affect students' academic experience. Furthermore, we seek to connect these perceptions to solutions.

TEACHERS' PERCEPTIONS OF SPEAKERS OF AAVE

C. A. Williams (2014) conducted research on the ways faculty perceive their students' ability to interpret social cues at a predominantly Black institution (PBI). This included faculty's perception of their students' ability to communicate using SE. This qualitative study focused on teachers of African American students and applied a discourse analysis to analyze participants' responses to the interview questions. As part of that study, faculty were asked about their students' literacy skills. This work gets at the heart of communicative expectations held by not only individual faculty members, but also the expectations held by academia in general and how those expectations are communicated.

It is worth noting, as an aside, that many educators have challenged the term "Standard English" for referring to mainstream White language because to label something as "standard" implies that anything outside of it is "not standard." Paris and Alim (2014) have suggested calling SE "Dominant American English" (DAE), as they assert that much of the research and discussion in the area of teaching speakers of AAVE is rooted in getting those students to use language practices more like those of White middle-class folks. We want our students to sound like and be themselves, but we know that we need to be explicit with our students about how society perceives them based on language use. Through the challenges and the debates, SE prevails as the "standard" means of communicating, especially in higher education.

Williams's 2014 study provided a treasure trove of faculty statements regarding their perceptions of students' ability to interpret social cues and use SE when expected. Here we examine the feedback that faculty provided, with an emphasis on contextualization and social literacy.

The first statement that we'll examine is that of a foreign language professor who stated, "In general, when they come to the office it is important to communicate with your instructor in a language I can understand. Since we are in an academic setting they have to use a certain discourse" (C. A. Williams, 2014, p. 138).

If we take a moment to underline the social cues the instructor provided in her response, it would look something like this: "In general, when they come to the office it is important to communicate with your instructor in a language I can understand. *Since we are in an academic setting they have to use a certain discourse.*" The instructor is simply stating that the setting/environment has already established the expected and accepted language, which is SE. However, she has done this in an implicit way. Furthermore, this is not a conversation held with students, but the expectation is used to shape a perception of the student.

Using the words, "a certain discourse" assumes that it is understood that college requires SE. In this case, the language the instructor "can understand" is SE. Also embedded in this comment is a perception of students who perform either inside or outside of this expectation. Those who perform outside of this expectation are using a language she cannot understand, and the onus is on the *students* to adapt to her understanding, rather than the other way around. She says "it is important to communicate with your instructor in a language I can understand" rather than "it is important to communicate with your students in a language they can understand." As queried by Paris and Alim (2017), "What if the goal of teaching and learning with youth of color was not ultimately to see how closely students could perform White middle-class norms, but rather was to explore, honor, extend, and at times, problematize their cultural practices and investments?" (p. 3).

There is another example provided by an English faculty member in her response to a question about students' use of language in academic settings. Like a piece of tapestry, the thread reemerges at the surface—explicitly, rather than the implicit messaging of the foreign language instructor:

> They are challenged. Many do not have Standard English spoken at home. Makes it difficult for them to code-switch. As a kid I watched my parents switch. Many students do not have access to that type of modeling. It is difficult

for younger students to do it and understand that it is constant practice. They are not hearing [it] when they leave the class. Difference in home literacy values. (C. A. Williams, 2014, p. 140)

These two faculty members are both teachers of language (English/literature and a foreign language), but they describe the language their students use in different ways. In the first example, AAVE is described as something the teacher cannot understand, and the result of students not reading the social context and not utilizing social literacy skills to help with their reading of the space. In the second, AAVE is described as a home language, with the student needing support to manage SE in the academic setting. These descriptions are powerful when considering how they actually communicate a perception about the student, their language, and even the way literacy is valued in their homes.

As teachers, we have the potential to pass these perceptions to students through our interactions with them and through the ways we attempt to help them understand how they are perceived by society's power brokers. Even more alarming is that few students know and understand that this is happening around them.

In our discussions with colleagues, we talk about how our African American students respond to certain teachers. For African American faculty, it has been disheartening when they receive low evaluations from students and White faculty receive high evaluations. It is concerning because some of the basis of the evaluation is students' perceptions of African American faculty as having unreasonably high expectations of them with regard to the quality of work the students submit and the way students "act" in class.

An academic advisor described the ways students labeled teachers when selecting courses. He stated that White and other non–African American teachers were seen as "cool." When he asked why, the students stated that the teachers did not "trip," but some of these teachers had been the doorway dwellers described in the introduction of this book. They did not explicitly "trip" in their direct interactions with the students, but they still held perceptions of these students as being unable to perform certain tasks due to poor academic preparation and their use of AAVE. On the other hand, the academic advisor shared that in his conversations with the African American faculty, they communicated a belief that their students were intellectually capable and able to perform any task placed before them, but were frustrated with the way non–African American faculty "played both sides" when it came to the students.

In Williams's study, a White teacher stated that she deflects when a student performs in a way that is not considered acceptable. Another White male teacher used the term "ghetto" to describe the way an African American

Dean's List student spoke, while a White female teacher described that same student's language as being thick with AAVE (C. A. Williams, 2014). In this same academic setting, White students' language was seldom the topic of conversation even when they did not strictly use SE. Even when White students use informal language, it is still more closely aligned to SE in ways AAVE is not (Young, 2004).

What students do not realize is that the same teacher they describe as "cool" is the one who holds damaging perceptions of them that are communicated in department meetings, in discussions about internship opportunities, and when contacted for recommendations. Students make the mistake of asking these teachers for support and letters of recommendation.

To offer balance to the discussion, faculty were then asked how they respond to students who demonstrate a limited command of the expected academic discourse. A faculty member said,

> I tend to be a little more provocative in class . . . I let them know that depending on the venue, they need to be mindful of how they are communicating and the receivers of the message. Because depending on the language that they use, they may give others permission to use that language that is unintended and so they need to be mindful about unintended consequences of their communication. (C. A. Williams, 2014, p. 207)

Another faculty member said,

> There is this thing I have students read. I use it as an opportunity to discuss how this person would be perceived. Because the tone is very hostile and there are over 60 errors. I ask them what impression would this give.. . . . Use activities to help students conceptualize what communication means to perception. (C. A. Williams, 2014, p. 141)

What also came out of this discussion was the idea that, when participating in the types of reflective activities such as the one described earlier, students' perceptions of AAVE are critical and almost mirror teachers' perceptions, as if these perceptions have been passed on to them in some way. This leads us to take the position that students are aware of the differences between the language they use, AAVE, and the language they are expected to use, SE. However, they are challenged by *how* to navigate between the two languages. For some students, the switch is about changing the pitch or tone of their voices.

As an African American male student in English composition stated during a discussion about SE, "It is like talking to a White person." Therefore, SE is aligned with whiteness, and African American students understand that they *should* or are *expected* to talk to White people in a different way than they talk to each other. This reflects an embedded, historically rooted practice that whiteness deserves differences. SE is elevated as the "standard" and, by extension, so is whiteness. Because of this, we must reflect on the ways our students interact with whiteness and how that might influence their use of or resistance to SE, their perceptions of SE and AAVE, and the ways we reinforce this in our classrooms.

Students also hold some of the same perceptions, stereotypes, and judgments of their language as held by mainstream society. This leaves us, as teachers, at a crossroad. We are faced with the task of ensuring that our students leave our classrooms ready to meet the demands and expectations of the mainstream society, but without further damaging their intellectual, cultural, and community esteem. Again, we don't want our students to be seen as imposters in the academic setting or when they look in the mirror.

ADDRESSING STUDENTS' PERCEPTIONS OF AAVE

An example of students' perceptions of AAVE became evident through an activity that we designed for freshmen writing courses. Charles Chesnutt, Loraine Hansberry, Zora Neale Hurston, August Wilson, and other authors are often used in classes to expose students to African American writers and to help them identify and respond to issues facing their communities. This provides them with the opportunity to respond to texts that may represent a familiar experience and voice, as these texts represent parts of Black life using AAVE.

These authors discuss Black working- and middle-class quandaries (such as what to do with inheritances and how to divide family property). One example is Charles Chesnutt's *The Wife of His Youth*. This story examines class, colorism, racial passing, and moral obligation as central themes. After reading the text, students voiced what was almost disbelief about the language used by the characters in the book. The following is a sample from the text:

> "My name's 'Liza,'" she began, "'Liza Jane.' W'en I wuz young I us'ter b'long ter Marse Bob Smif, down in ole Missoura. I wuz bawn down dere. W'en I wuz a gal I wuz married ter a man named Jim. But Jim died, an' after dat I married a merlatter man named Sam Taylor. Sam wuz free-bawn, but his mammy and daddy died, an' de w'ite folks 'prenticed him ter my marster fer ter work fer 'im 'tel he wuz growed up. Sam worked in de fiel', an' I wuz de cook. One day Ma'y Ann, ole miss's maid, came rushin' out ter de kitchen, an' says she, 'Liza Jane, ole marse gwine sell yo' Sam down de ribber.'" (Chesnutt, 1899, p. 5)

Students' initial response to the printed text was that it was written in a language they did not understand (which sounds like the foreign language professor from C. A. Williams, 2014). After discussion, it became apparent that students did not make a connection between the language they use while speaking and the language they were seeing in print. As mentioned in Williams's (2014) work, they viewed the language as a deficiency. Some students even went as far as to say that Liza, the character who used AAVE, was ignorant.

After further discussion about Mr. Ryder's response to Liza Jane's sudden appearance, some students actually stated that Mr. Ryder should not reveal himself as Sam Taylor, Liza Jane's husband who left with a promise to return and purchase her freedom, because he shouldn't want to be associated with her. Essentially, students agreed that Liza Jane's language would act as a hindrance to Mr. Ryder/Sam Taylor's hopes for upward social mobility. Nowhere in the story are the readers privy to Liza Jane's intellectual abilities; however, the assumption, based on her verbal language, was that she was ignorant and deficient. This also occurred when reading other works that used dialect.

It became apparent that students' perceptions of AAVE were closely aligned to mainstream ideas that it is "less than" or "not standard." It is important to remember that these students primarily speak AAVE themselves. However, when pushed to transcribe their speech (spelling out what they hear when they speak), they were able to see that there was not much difference between the way they speak and the words they were judging in print. This example is provided here because as teachers, we have to be cautious about the way we enact our perceptions of students based on their use of language in our classrooms. We should want to create a space where education is preservative.

Students' Perceptions of AAVE

Students' reactions to reading and seeing AAVE in print demonstrates that they judge the language similar to the ways that teachers judge the language. It also communicates somewhat of a misunderstanding about AAVE, its history, and its structure. Some students only know that the way they communicate has provided them with success in their day-to-day lives. They miss the important lesson about context.

When teachers make judgments, it may have implications for students' academic experience and, to an extent, their academic esteem. One of the complaints we hear students make about writing is that they don't know how to say what they mean. However, their work reveals that they have a difficult time using the concise wording that is expected in academic settings. They rely heavily on the use of examples and other context-specific language and descriptions that echo the concern of the foreign language instructor in Williams's (2014) study.

The messages that students have received about AAVE generally focus on its qualities as deficiencies. Students either embody that message and try to avoid using it, or they resist, and messages about ways to move in and out of various discourse communities are lost. These students feel that we are trying to force them to reject the very spaces that they associate with love and comfort and, as a result, they choose not to reject love and comfort for assimilation. For that reason, our messages around language must be sure to include representations of *how* to maintain our primary discourse while developing another one.

WHAT'S THE PROBLEM WITH WRITING THE WAY I TALK?

I am a black woman poet and I sound like one.

—Lucille Clifton

During a recent conference focused on African American life, a young African American female graduate student, attending a presentation examining African American students' experiences in predominantly White academic spaces, shared her experiences around language use. She said that she has always been told by her mostly White teachers that the problem with her writing is that she writes the way she talks. A member of the panel addressed this comment by saying, "You should have asked the person, what's wrong with the way I talk? They write the way they talk."

Teachers (both African American and White) have said this same thing to so many African American students since their writing skills emerged. Writing and other ways of communicating are seen as an extension and demonstration of thinking. Telling a student that "the problem with your writing is that you write the way you talk" is like saying there is a problem with the way you think, and the way you think has been damaged by the community you come from and the things you have experienced. This leads to reduced academic and self-esteem. Some will argue that White students are often told not to write the way they talk, for example, in meandering sentences full of fillers; but this tends to be an admonishment to refine the written form of their acceptable native language, not to abandon their native language altogether.

According to Steele (1997; 2003), the longer African Americans stay in school, regardless of social class, the more they tend to suffer from a decline in success in school, even at the college level. The messages students receive from their teachers is one that reinforces their place in what Mike Rose (1990) calls "on the boundary." For too many African American students, it becomes an exhausting tightrope act that they, or the institutions in which they enroll, decide is too much to continue. They find themselves leaving either without what they came for—a degree—or leaving with the degree, but also with built-up frustration from years of trying to meet a moving target. This frustration emerges as confrontation and an overall dislike for the academic community and the discourse associated with it.

Teacher education programs have traditionally promoted a sort of color-blind approach to teaching. We hear teachers say things like, "I don't see color" or "I just see students," but the truth is we see and we hear culture, gender, and social class more than we would like to admit. We are not fooling anyone with these well-intentioned statements, and our students know it, too. They know it when we say things like, "The problem with your writing is that you write the way you talk." This is not a statement made only by non–African American teachers; African American teachers use this to help students understand that, in theory, there should be difference between the way they speak casually and the way they speak in professional and formal settings. However, that is not always the message that is received.

Welcoming AAVE in the Classroom

In Young's (2004) examination of the language of an African American male student in a freshman composition class, he sought to identify the connection between language, power, culture, and student success in environments where mainstream discourse is dominant (and expected). Young was interested in discovering if the student would be more successful in his class if he did not feel intimidated by what Gutierrez, Rymes, and Larson (1995) call *teacher script*. Essentially, Young (2004) was attempting to create the third space that Gutierrez and colleagues (1995) examined in their study of language in the classroom.

The student was encouraged to use his primary language, AAVE, in speaking in class and in writing essays. Young (2004) considered the work of Campbell (1997), Delpit (1995a), Gilyard (1999), and Smitherman (1977, 1995, 2000) when deciding to encourage the use of AAVE and when reflecting on the possible implications this decision had on the student, the other students in the class, and his own teaching practices. The African American male student did show increased confidence in his writing ability; however, he was also still at the school five years later. Young (2004) wondered if he had hurt the student more than helped him by failing to prepare him to communicate in mainstream contexts, something that his other teachers would expect.

Responding to AAVE in the Classroom

Young's work provides a start to a rich discussion and possibly a point of consideration for teachers faced with a similar situation. Do we allow speakers of AAVE to use this language in spaces that we as teachers know will expect SE? As practitioners, we are faced with this struggle. Students have every right to communicate in a language that is comfortable to them, but in cases where the expectation has economic and social implications, we have to be open and honest with our students about perception and help them read the context in the same way we teach them to read print texts.

Delpit (1995a, 1995b), Ladson-Billings (1994, 2002, 2005), Moje (2007), Smitherman (1977, 1994/2000, 1995, 2000), Steele (1997, 2003), and Young (2004) all speak to the ways mainstream contexts may view students of color as deficient. In regard to language, Smitherman (1977, 1994/2000, 1995, 2000) speaks to the idea that language regarded as outside of the mainstream is considered deficient. Moreover, a deficient label carries with it the idea that the person using the language is deficient, and that the culture of that language is deficient.

The classroom space is likely to be a microcosm of the larger society. If schools, specifically classrooms, function as spaces where teachers socialize students, then one could expect students to enter with schemata that serve them well in this cultural model. However, what happens when socialization does not take place? What happens when teachers do not see this task as their responsibility? Students may in fact find that they constantly fail the tests that are administered by the classroom space itself, and they may become withdrawn or frustrated.

Overall, teachers' perceptions of students drive their interactions with students. Also, teachers' perceptions of themselves drive how they approach teaching, and how their teaching impacts students' learning. The faculty-student interaction can be a "psychological drama," as Brookfield (1986) puts it. When considering culture and the social implications for language, some faculty members may not be willing to take the risk when it comes to explicitly discussing the implications of behavior and language with students, because (1) they do not realize that their colleagues are walking the same tightrope, and (2) they do not feel armed with the tools to begin to approach such a sensitive topic with their students.

REFLECTION

We started this process wanting to know more about the ways that enacting basic discourse expectations impacts success in college and beyond for

African American students. We started this process focusing on literacy in general, and moved to language use and perceptions of it. Of course, that was a broad idea and needed refining. The narrowing process required us to think deeply and get to the root of what we really wanted to know and our ideas about it. After much thought, we realized that

1. Our ideas about literacy were very different from the way literacy is traditionally defined as the basic ability to read and write.
2. When we referred to "literacy," what we really are talking about is the way literacy is enacted in context-specific ways.
3. When we referred to "impact," we were talking about the consequences of not displaying context-expected or context-specific literacy acts.

Often, perceptions about one's thinking ability are conceived before any interaction with one's reading or writing ability. And perceptions about thinking capacity and ability may lead to perceptions about social class. These perceptions may influence opportunity and access to opportunity.

A review of the literature led us to think about language and literacy more broadly. We also continued to listen to the conversations, at the college level, about students' skills. What we realized is that, for teachers, students' writing was the easiest place to point to as evidence of poor preparation for college, poor communication skills, and an inability to think critically or transfer knowledge. It was a safe place for teachers because it provided concrete evidence—writing samples—that they believed supported their perceptions about a particular group of students.

Criticizing students' writing is also safer for teachers, because to criticize students' verbal interactions might be uncomfortable; the teacher may be perceived as judging the students' culture as inadequate (Alim & Smitherman, 2012; Delpit, 1995a, 1995b, 2002; Lindquist & Seitz, 2008; Smitherman, 1977). To say that the student entered an instructor's office with his pants "sagging" may be judgmental based on the way young men with sagging pants are portrayed (Young, 2004). If so, an instructor adopts a perception about a student before the student either provided a piece of writing or opened his mouth, and that perception is reinforced when the student speaks using a language other than what is expected, SE.

When faculty members say that students do not write well, they are able to point directly to instances when they experienced students' literacy skills in a way they considered to be outside of their expectations, without running the risk of being culturally insensitive. What faculty members do not want to say—even if it is exactly what they think—is that African American urban students lack the necessary skills, both academic and social, to meet their expectations, and that they arrived at this conclusion based on the ways these students, or other students who look like them, speak, dress, and act in college.

In addition, faculty members may not want to say that African American urban students lack the necessary skills to meet their expectations because of the way the students act at home and in their communities. But, in essence, that is exactly what they said. Just because one does not say it, does not mean that one does not think it and act on it.

Here we provide an entry point into a sensitive topic. Faculty do not always feel armed with strategies to address students concerning the realities of particular behavior. This feeling is similar to Delpit's (1995a) discussion in which she adds that teachers who consider themselves progressive and informed may feel that, by pushing students who are considered to be from minority backgrounds to learn and use the dominant discourse, they are actually further oppressing those students. However, Delpit (1995a) also states that when we are not clear with our students about the impact of perceptions, we are actually working to ensure that the obstacles related to discourse remain intact. In essence, we have the playbook, but we are not sharing it with those who need it most.

Chapter 3

Closing the Gap

Connecting Students and Partnering AAVE and Collegiate Composition

Let's suppose you are interested in taking tango lessons. A key bit of coaching advice would be to "breathe and glide." Observations of the dance have revealed that there is also a very slight pause at the end of each glide. We can posit that this combination is a bit like the legitimizing of the AAVE in academic circles.

First, there was the emergence of scholarly debate about the evolution and validity of AAVE. This was followed by intense research into its linguistic nature, work that is still being done. The challenge to school systems to include AAVE in their teaching methodologies resulted in the Ann Arbor lawsuit, filed by parents on behalf of their children enrolled in public school. The Ann Arbor decision preceded the most well-known legal and political wrangling over AAVE—the Oakland Ebonics debate.

In the wake of Oakland, there was a huge exhale as educators and scholars gathered courage, chutzpah, and evidence to argue for the validity and inclusion of AAVE in public education. Then, as the argument wound its way through boards of education, there was a moment or two of gliding as the AAVE proponents gained traction and espied a victory. But then, there was the inevitable pause—now that its legitimacy was no longer an issue, what would be the practical applications?

There has been some progress (the proliferation of AAVE-based children's literature as well as the development of some instructional materials for elementary schools are cases in point). But the use of AAVE in the halls of higher learning is hit or miss. It is the intention of this chapter to take another breath and glide into a discussion of why and how the use of AAVE in college introductory composition courses for certain demographics is not only warranted, but essential. First, we review the definitions of Black English (or AAVE) and recap the twenty-year-old Ebonics discussion. So, deep breath in, and get ready to glide.

[RE]DEFINING AAVE AND ITS ROOTS

Geneva Smitherman has proffered a definition of AAVE that we will use as the foundation for discussion: "a set of communication patterns and practices ... that form a rule-governed language system ... resulting from Africans' appropriation and transformation of a foreign tongue during the African Holocaust ... as they struggled to combine the cultures of Africa and the United States" (1994/2000, p. 19). For when one considers the birth of AAVE or Black English, one must begin with inclusion of the slavery experience, and all its permutations, in the formation of the AAVE speech community. Such an understanding is supported by the work of Dell Hymes (1974), whose use of research on the components of speech defines the speech community as the social unit of analysis.

A social unit, of course, is the basic building block of society or community or civilization. Many speakers of AAVE are dominant building blocks in their communities. Even those Black people who reside within the boundaries of White neighborhoods are familiar with at least some aspects of AAVE. Black language evolved with the cultural progress of Black people in the United States; it is specifically tied to the presence of popular cultural references.

And yet speakers of Black language must also learn to speak Standard English (SE) or, in the case of the postsecondary student, college English. English composition classes must help speakers of AAVE not only to learn to speak SE fluently, but to distinguish between appropriate audiences and messaging prompts for its usage. In other words, in their bi-dialectical-ness, they have to be aware of the rules observed by speech communities to which they do not belong, even as they are immersed in an educational system that is free to ignore the linguistic rules of their own variety of English.

Characteristics of Black English

It can be argued that Zora Neale Hurston was among the first to bring attention to this thing called Black language, the phenomenon also known as AAVE. Her essay, "Characteristics of Negro Expression," published in 1934, serves as a stepping-off point for this discussion of AAVE. In that essay, Hurston delineates specific features of AAVE and their purpose in the "Negro" cultural context, making a strong case for the appreciation of the grammatical features of the Negro's forms of expressions.

For example, in her essay, Hurston (1934/1994) points to the Negro's need to adorn—the tendency to fancy up language so as to approximate the language of the so-called educated White:

> The primitive man exchanges descriptive words. His terms are all close fitting. Frequently the Negro, even with detached words in his vocabulary—not evolved in him, but transplanted on his tongue by contact—must do. So we have "chop axe", "sitting-chair", "cook-pot" and the like because the speaker has in his mind the picture of the object in use. Action. Everything is illustrated. So we can say the White man thinks in a written language while the Black man thinks in hieroglyphics. (p. 39)

This statement alludes to the tensions inherent in oral communication for the Black man and woman in the United States.

Excluded from any form of written communication from the time of their arrival in this country, Black folk developed their own forms of oral communication, combining remnants of retained native languages with conceptually phrased understandings of their new environs (popular culture references) to come up with the first embodiments of Black language. According to Smitherman (2000, p. 33), "common language evolved because the Africans share two linguistic denominators: the English vocabulary and the structure and meaning systems of the African languages."

In the context of the Harlem Renaissance with its collaboration between White owners of cultural production and the burgeoning Black discussion of the nature of Black life, to say nothing of the continued attempts by researchers to devalue AAVE, Hurston served as a breath of fresh air. Her essay applied a definition of originality, value, and worth to the dialects of the southern Blacks that she studied; dialects that were indeed precursors to what we now call Black English or AAVE.

And so, Black English emerges as "a counter-ideology; it [becomes] the language of rebellion and the symbolic solidarity among the oppressed" (Smitherman, 2000, p. 108). It became and remains the lingua franca of da hood, a fall-back dialect for many corporate Blacks when returning home for the holidays, and a continuation of a special code for conversing among the Black speech community. But does it have a place in public education? If so, what is that place, and how can it be carved out? Suggesting answers to these and other questions around AAVE or Black English is the aim of this text.

Resolving Tensions with AAVE

On December 18, 1996, the Oakland Board of Education adopted a resolution on Ebonics (the prevailing terminology for Black English, coined from combining *ebony* with *phonics*) and its relationship to the school system. The preamble stated unequivocally that "African Language Systems are genetically based and not a dialect of English" (Oakland Board of Education, 1996, n.p.). Significantly, the resolution situated its definitions of African languages as among those of West and Niger-Congo Africa.

The resolution alluded to California legislation that, though repeatedly vetoed, "recognized the unique language stature of descendants of slaves" [as well as the existence of] "court mandated educational programs that have substantially benefitted African American children [in other states] in the interest of vindicating their equal protection of the law rights under the 14th Amendment to the United States Constitution."

The resolution concluded that the Board "officially recognizes the existence and cultural and historic bases of West and Niger-Congo African Language Systems and each language as the predominantly primary language of African American students." The practical application, however, was a bit vague: "Devise and implement the best possible academic program for imparting instruction to African American students in their primary language" (Oakland Board of Education, 1996, n.p.).

The resolution was immediately controversial. Without rehashing the specific points of the controversy as it existed then, the relevance to the argument about speech community, home language, and incorporation of AAVE (the compromise name that grew out of opposition to Ebonics) rests on two legs: the embedded assumption of inferiority in the Oakland resolution, and the substitution of "dialect" for "language" in the argument.

The assumption of a communicative skill inferiority is explicitly referenced in the original language of the resolution by allusions to Limited English Proficiency (LEP) and Non-English Proficiency (NEP). The definition of Ebonics as another language to be addressed by "special education" reinforced the idea of pathology.

When and Where We Speak

Languages are defined by specific characteristics: morphology, phonology, lexicon, and syntax. A contributing factor to the controversy of the Oakland decision was its waffling on the question of language versus dialect. AAVE is, as Taylor Jones's (2014, n.p.) doctoral research indicates, a "full-fledged dialect of English, just like say British English. It is entirely rule bound—meaning it has very clear grammar that can be and is described in great detail. It is not simply 'ungrammatical.' If you do not conform to the grammar of AAVE, the result is ungrammatical sentences in AAVE."

Why, you say, would one continue the discussion about AAVE's viability with a 2014 doctoral student's blog when the point was made in the original

Oakland resolution, and has been demonstrated articulately by the superlative and pioneering scholarly work of Dr. Geneva Smitherman and others? Because the point is being stressed by today's generation of students and newly minted PhDs.

The spoken word TED Talk by Dr. Jamila Lyiscott (2014) on the three Englishes she speaks—AAVE, Jamaican patois, and SE—is a searing affirmation of the validity of AAVE. Likewise is the poet Kai Davis's language-alert piece titled *F*ck I Look Like!!!!* (2012), which slams the diminishing of AAVE descriptors: "You say gargantuan. I say big as shit."

These young women bear witness to Wheeler and Swords (2004), who assert that "the child who speaks in a vernacular dialect is not making language errors; instead, he or she is speaking correctly in the language of the home discourse community" (p. 471). *Good afternoon* belongs in the community of Standard English. *Whassup*, or sometime just the nonverbal equivalent of an upward nod of the head, is the lingua franca of da hood. And to be fluent in both is an advantage. It is our contention that teachers of urban students, K–12 and postsecondary, also should be fluent in both languages. More on that strategy later.

For now, let's examine where we are in the application of AAVE, considering Smitherman's work, and in direct reference to the freshman college composition classrooms made up of first-generation, urban students. Has our development in this regard been arrested at the time stamped by Smitherman's lexical dictionary of AAVE? And if so, how do we move forward from that place?

Language or Dialect

As mentioned, a stumbling block to forward movement after the Oakland decision was a debate about whether AAVE is a language or a dialect. Most problematic in settling this debate was the prevailing definition of dialect as it related to class. For example, some thought Black English was the purview entirely of the working class (Batan & Smitherman, 1983). Some ethnographers posited that Black English "was the lingo of criminals, dope pushers, [and] teen hoodlums" (Smitherman, 2000, p. 84).

The class distinction gave purchase to those who argued that any form of English spoken by Blacks in America was illegitimate, and thus unworthy of further consideration. The Oakland resolution tacitly supported this point of view when it failed to make a distinction between language and dialect. In retrospect, the discourse around this distinction was a major point of contention among African American scholars.

And while Carol Reed's (1973) opinion essay—written, in its initial form, over twenty years before the Oakland resolution—is soundly convincing of the need to define and consider AAVE as a dialectical form of English, albeit with its own set of grammar rules, there is a parallel need to do away with the class-bound definition of the word *dialect*. Or at least, as Smitherman (2000) points out, a need to realize that some other speakers of English are actually speaking a particular dialect. In fact, SE (sometimes referred to as Language of Wider Communication [LWC]), because of its dominance as the language of literacy, commerce, politics, and education (Smitherman, 2000, p. 38), is defined as a class dialect spoken by American power elites. This classification is contrasted with the nonstandard English spoken by working-class whites.

What distinguishes Black English is that it is a "racial dialect" (Smitherman 2000). That is, it is spoken across the African American class system. In 1997, the Linguistics Society of America proffered a description that can be used to satisfy supporters of the racial argument as well as those who want to stick to their dialect guns: "African American English is a legitimate and systematic language variety of English . . . [known] as Ebonics, AAVE, and Vernacular Black English and by other names it is systematic and rule-governed like all natural speech varieties" (Lee, 2007, p. 83).

William Labov (1972) actually went further, stating that African American English *is* a structured language, and not a version of English. Chomsky (1988/2004) seems to tie it all together by linking language to communication and a "biological nature [that] creates a kind of social space, to place itself in interaction with other people" (p. 369). And so, it is upon the phrase *variety of English* that we will place further definitions of Black English.

Teaching AAVE

Carol Reed's work represents an approach to teaching Black English from the perspective that dialect equals variety, and that AAVE can be taught without socioeconomic aspersions. Her (1973) work draws on the performance of students enrolled in the Brooklyn College English-as-a-Second-Dialect (ESD) curriculum. The curriculum's objective was achievement of the "ability to discriminate Black English Vernacular features and instances of cross-dialectal interference in their writing, and the ability to translate these into their appropriate Standard English equivalent" (pp. 289–90). In other words, how and when to code-switch.

Reed's research offers a rubric for how to reach this state of fluency. She emphasizes how a certain amount of what she called "de-brainwashing" was required and especially critical to the achievement of the adult AAVE speaker. The de-brainwashing that Reed refers to is a phenomenon that encompasses the AAVE speaker's awareness of differences in her speech pattern from those of so-called educated people, coupled with a learned sense that her speech patterns are inferior.

Reed argues that the student and non-AAVE-speaking teachers (more on them later) "must be helped toward an appreciation of [this] native dialect as a unique and valid linguistic system" (1973, p. 290) in accord with the rhetorical foundations of SE. To put it another way, AAVE not only has a linguistic philosophy, but can, as Jones (2014) points out, say some things better than Standard English, a point made by Hurston (1934/1994). Hurston might argue that the tendency usually comes out as the more expressive way of communicating.

Carol Lee (2007) puts this phenomenon of validating AAVE another way: "Privileging AAVE is a way to access the intrinsic knowledge of students" (p. 91). First-generation, urban college students in particular are so much smarter than they are often given credit for. While they may not have the vocabulary to articulate the "belief systems, epistemologies, practices and ways of using language" (Lee, 2007, p. 14) that are associated with SE, the use of their own variety of English in no way proclaims deficits that make them uneducable.

In fact, most of these students have prior knowledge that the teacher does not (Lee, 2007). Navigating neighborhood turf boundaries requires skills of negotiation and diplomacy that equip some of these young people for careers in foreign affairs; to be completely truthful, in addition to the balancing acts required in their neighborhoods, Black urban students must navigate the world of the dominant culture. And so Lee proposes the use of *cultural data sets* [her term] "to provide [students] with a language to talk about their problem-solving processes" (2007, p. 61).

Cultural data sets are texts that students are familiar with from everyday life. Once the selected familiar text is coupled with an interpretive problem— composing a claim for an argumentative paper—it becomes easier for the student to learn how to do something. A simple example serves to illustrate this point.

The traditional three-paragraph essay for a claim requires the development of a thesis statement and the addition of supporting evidence. One of the major problems AAVE-speaking students have with this assignment has to do with how they process communication. Remembering Hurston's focus on "the will to adorn," we can understand the wandering way in which students approach adding evidence to support their claim. Three paragraphs do not allow room for a wandering approach.

The pivot move in basketball (an example of a cultural data set) becomes instructive in how to frame one's evidence. In the pivot, the teacher might explain, the player may turn in any direction she likes, but one foot must stay planted in place. This is the same with a thesis and a thread of supporting evidence. The writer is free to search widely, as long as the supporting statement is firmly anchored in the thesis statement.

This, the teacher might continue, is the work of a transition. The writer is keeping her thesis or main point in the forefront of her essay (the foot that is planted and immobile), but she is also free to make additional points (through moving the other foot). This basketball analogy was a tool to provide students a way of, as Lee writes, "making connections between what they already do and what they are expected to do"; for, as she continues, the object of teaching is to establish "habits of mind" and to promote an environment where "intellectual risk taking is a [safe] norm for class participation" (Lee, 2007, pp. 60–61).

Teaching strategies of empowerment are also revealed when returning to the work of Carol Reed. Her presentation of an AAVE curriculum (1973) is built on teaching the "rationale" behind linguistic choices made in both AAVE and SE. There is an inherent logic in both varieties, and the presentation of the source and context of the logic goes a long way toward eliminating any sense of "doing as I do" simply because "I said so"—a reality commonly understood as "regurgitate what the teacher said."

The following mini-lesson is an example of understanding the logic of why the phrase *could of* is incorrect. Learning any language or variety thereof is partially based on hearing it spoken. Coupled with the AAVE speech community's unique pronunciation patterns, the phrase "could *have*" might be heard as "could *of*" and the error thus becomes one of mishearing rather than one of an innate linguistic inability. Explaining the point in this way, elicited a favorite student phrase: *Oh!* (translation: *I see* or *I understand now* or *I get it*).

Self-assessment by the instructor is a critical factor in creating successful learning environments for AAVE-speaking college students. Such self-knowledge is essential to the creation of assessments that elevate the variety of English that students speak, while making a case for the acquisition of a second variety, Standard English. We must, as Asa Hillard exhorted, ensure that our children have access to educators who "are not puzzled by how to teach them" (quoted in Lee, 2007, p. 112). How well teachers are able to speak the English variety of their students will determine how well they are able to manage communicating SE to students who don't speak it, let alone accustomed to reasoning in it.

And in composition especially, but in college in general, the ability to reason is job one. The parallel of TOEFL/TESOL (Test of English as a Foreign Language/Teaching English to Speakers of Other Languages) pedagogy is instructive. One would not staff an English as a Second Language course with a person who couldn't speak the second language. The methodology of learning is built around the exchange of two languages. This state of affairs is as it should be in the teaching of so-called Standard English to those who are fluent in another version. In their world, *their* version is standard.

And so, the first need is for teachers who can easily code-switch into the language of the home discourse community, and who understand the political ramifications of empowerment through language. According to Chomsky (1988/2004, p. 574), when one knows a language or a variety of it, one has "mastered a system of rules and principles." It follows that one cannot master the system if one doesn't know the language. It is like being told to dress for tennis, only to arrive at the venue and find that the team is dressed for basketball.

The balancing of the home discourse language with the ever-present White standard (as privileged in tests and texts) softens the antagonism that often surfaces during class discussions. And class discussions are perhaps more important with first-generation urban college students, as their learning style leans toward the use of oral language.

As linguists teach, language learning begins with hearing the language spoken. Through listening, a child acquires the regular rules of the grammar and overgeneralizes them (Fromkin, Rodman, & Hyams, 2002). This is why the toddler learning to speak English is not incorrect when she says *I goed to the park with Daddy*. Her construction is a result of learning that the past tense is created by adding *-ed*. What the child hasn't learned yet are the exceptions.

Our students similarly tend to sound pedantic as well as grammatically incorrect when in the novice stage of practicing marketplace English. Part of the challenge is the subject matter of the material being assigned. How often it is of close interest to the student? More often than not, some curriculum specialist (probably not a speaker of AAVE) chose the text for reasons related to a context familiar to him—current events of interest to him, or a topic deemed by the dominant culture to be of interest to the general population.

But what exactly is the general population? A basic aspect of all problem solving is pattern recognition (Lee, 2007). Reading is of course a form of problem solving in that it requires applying contextual clues to the author's word choices: "These contextual clues signal to the [readers] what kind of activity this is, what people do here, how people talk, what people do. The features that are relatively routine in a familiar setting are what help us to recognize it as such and construct our own understanding of our relationship to that setting" (Gumperz & Hymes, 1972, quoted in Lee, 2007, p. 81).

We understand that recognizing settings and contexts (patterns) assist us in making sense of what we read, while simultaneously acquiring new words to add to our vocabulary. Unfortunately, much of the reading that first-generation, college student speakers of AAVE encounter is not at all familiar. And so, time is wasted in an effort to decode the contexts rather than discerning meaning from the text in its entirety.

Reading aloud has been a go-to corrective for learning the language of Standard English. But reading aloud doesn't go far enough. There is no connection, no pause to consider the meaning of what is being read. And understanding the logic of Standard English, understanding *why* something is phrased in a particular way, is critical to mastery of the form. Robust class discussions can address this issue when the instructor can (1) break down the AAVE sentence/idea into its component parts, (2) code-switch or transliterate into marketplace English, and (3) compare the logic in each case.

Not only do students get practice with hearing Standard English oral expression while comparing that version with their home discourse language, but talking in the two varieties helps with their writing. Because students think in their home discourse language, discussions—in the vein that is being examined—better equips them to translate their thoughts onto paper. The value of textbooks that would mirror these kinds of discussions in AAVE and SE would be extremely significant.

"Why Do I Gotta Do This?"

Lee's concept of cultural data sets leads us to another extremely important aspect of teaching college-level composition: addressing the reality of why students attend college in the first place. What is the value of a college education today—not in terms of economics (though there is certainly a case to be made for that), but in the sense of the valuing the intrinsic worth of critical thinking and its application to everyday life?

College freshmen are frequently asked why they came to college. It is amazing how many first-generation urban students respond: "To get a good job." No matter that their definition of a good job is simply one that pays a lot of money. What is important is that they seem to make no connection between college and what is to be *learned*! Yet when quizzed about the connection, they are able to readily see the difference between the applicant who comes to a job interview with "Is y'all hi-ing today?" and the one who asks, "Are you taking applications?"

The different cultural messages inherent in these two questions, posed in differing variants of English, form the nexus of understanding the tensions that inhibit success in SE language use by first-generation, urban college students. Students are readily able to identify the first example as an inappropriate question for a job applicant. It is more difficult to unpack the connection between the phrase and the daily language they actually speak. And it is that connection that teaching composition with a focus on AAVE is meant to strengthen.

Now is the time for another pause on the dance cards of our two varieties of English, and the time for inserting a caveat. Throughout this discussion, the term *Standard English* has been employed to identify the particular variety endemic to the American academic marketplace. But use of this term must be taken with a grain of salt, not because the authors believe it to be universally normative but because, as earlier analysis has pointed out, context plus audience are the ultimate arbiters of what is *standard*.

The college classroom of the freshman composition course is where use of SE is de rigueur. The dance lessons—how and when to perform the code—are given here. Here is where the dance cards are filled out and where the partnership between AAVE and Standard English is forged. The classroom from which I have drawn examples is populated with adult, mostly first-generation college students who are fluent in AAVE and less so in this academic, marketplace English.

As mentioned earlier, a major objective of the freshman composition course is movement from the novice level to mastery of the codes of SE, including mastery of its rhetoric—the style of expository writing acceptable to users of the code. But what about the student whose advancement is hampered by dominance of a different "home language"? For, as Lee (2007, p. 21) points out, "the rhetorical impact and the aesthetics of how language is used are as important as the content of the message." Identification of rhetorical features of AAVE is part of understanding how, as Smitherman (2000, p. 61) writes, "language is used as a teaching/socializing force and as a means of establishing one's reputation via verbal competence."

The ability to establish one's reputation via verbal competence is a highly prized skill among speakers of AAVE. In the vernacular it is known as *signifying* and ranks among the top rhetorical features of AAVE. In summary, signifying is the "trash-talking" (insult-trading style of communication), that is a mainstay of everyday humor within the Black community (Rickford & Rickford, 2000). Other features include call and response; rhythmic, exaggerated, evocative, and dramatic language patterns; proverbial and aphoristic phrasing and word play; indirection and tonal semantics; spontaneity; and concreteness (Lee, 2007; Smitherman, 1977).

Hurston's 1934 essay delineates these features, and their presence has been noted by Smitherman and others writing about AAVE. While not directly related to the learning of the finer points of grammar and production of essays, the teacher of college composition with a classroom of speakers of AAVE, armed with an understanding of its linguistic features, has a definite advantage in understanding classroom behavior and engaging with these students.

For example, the tendency to speak aloud one's opinion, following the expression of opinion by a classmate, but without being formally recognized by the teacher, is not a form of disrespect, but rather evidence that the student is engaged. It is an active use of "call and response," a behavioral practice most often associated with the Black church, but one that also crops up in academic settings. The proper response would be, as Lee (2007) points out, for the teacher to summarize all of the seemingly random comments—transliterated in SE—for the benefit of collective understanding of the point in question.

The spontaneity of it all is also not lost. Both Chomsky (1988/2004) and Smitherman (2000) argue for a language pedagogy that privileges the utility of sociolinguistics and its focus on the social and ethnic features of language. The goal should be the achievement of a functional competence, rather than the mastery of surface structure compliance.

Continuing this line of reasoning requires some basic explanation of language structure, as defined by Chomskyan theories of linguistics. In the most simplistic terms, surface structure is understood to be the outward form of a sentence, and deep structure as an abstract representation that identifies the ways a sentence can be analyzed and interpreted. Chomsky (1988/2004, p. 127) defines these terms as descriptive of the "far reaching, deep-seated universal principles of language structure."

In other words, language is an intellectual construct that is connected to one's cognitive development, one's ability to make sense out of the world. According to Chomsky (1988/2004), this intellectual construct or language (and its varieties) is a "major feature of human cognitive organization that linguistics tries to characterize" (p. 367). And yet these intellectual constructs or structures are not learned. Chomsky credits their existence to genetic predispositions, giving rise to another specialized form of linguistics that he terms *biological linguistics*.

But what does all of this have to do with Black English? Well, for one thing, Chomsky's theories of language universals and genetics align quite nicely with Hurston's "Characteristics of Negro Expression." The characteristics she describes exist within the Black community across class lines and are accurately modeled by Chomsky's (1988/2004) pronouncement that "we [all] also think in terms of visual images . . . situations and events . . . many times we can't even begin to express in words what the content of our thinking is" (p. 368). And so, Hurston's citation of drama, the will to adorn, asymmetry, and originality in language is right on Chomsky's point.

But we have more work to do to codify the rules of Black English and educate teachers about them through textbooks. Proving that point is the underlying foundation of this text, and begs the need for academic texts that speak to this reality. As Smitherman (2000) explains, "It is critical that teachers have an understanding and appreciation for the language students bring to school [and de-emphasize] the emphasis on surface correctness . . . [there is] little or no emphasis on critical thinking and critical literacy" (p. 119). Failure to amend this approach is to inflict a grave injustice to speakers of AAVE and others, notably foreign students (more on these students later).

An example may help to illustrate the point. Much ado has been made of the frequent absence of the copula (the verb *to be*) in the formation of AAVE sentences in the present tense: *The man tall*. The form denotes a "recurring, habitual state of affairs" (Smitherman, 2000, p. 22). In spite of a "trend in English teaching in white middle-class schools [that] has been away from grammatical overkill and toward an emphasis on critical thinking," a college student whose essay contains consistently absent present tense forms of the verb *to be* is tasked with composing a "grammatically flawless piece" (Smitherman, 2000, p. 216).

The truth of the matter is that the deep structure meaning of the phrase *He tall* is equivalent to the SE phrase *He is tall*. The meaning in both cases is that *He is tall now and forever more*. Smitherman rightly asks the question: "After all, what do you want, good grammar or good sense?" (Smitherman, 2000, p. 124). She continues to expand this notion of good sense when it comes to evaluating speakers and writers of AAVE: "Language power is a function not of one's dialect [variety], but of larger linguistic structures used skillfully and effectively employed" (Smitherman, 2000, p. 124).

In other words, the most important aspect of an essay that contains the AAVE grammatical surface structure *He tall* is what the student is attempting to communicate about the tall one. Does the student have a functional competence in composition that permits her ideas to be understood?

The role of functional competence is further illustrated by the pedagogy applied in teaching English to speakers of foreign languages who are enrolled in American colleges and universities. ESL teaching techniques do not require students to master the fluency of native speakers of English, but to achieve this functional competence—the ability to successfully communicate an idea with increasing fluidity.

We argue that the establishment of AAVE as a variety of English rather than a different language does not necessarily negate the use of some ESL practices. I have had the opportunity to compare and contrast learning outcomes and successes within freshman composition classes taken by both speakers of English as a Second Language (ESL) and speakers of AAVE or English as a Second Dialect (ESD). For consideration, what follows is a brief synopsis of those experiences.

LYDIA'S CLASSROOM EXPERIENCE

The setting was a freshman English composition course, populated by both native speakers of English and a cohort of Chinese students who conversed among themselves in their Chinese dialects. The challenge was to transmit the codes of Standard English. The pedagogical approach—supported by the program director for rhetoric and composition—did not aim for student achievement of English language fluency, but the ability to read a text, formulate a point of view about the text, and compose a cogent argument supporting that point of view. This is the standard we were targeting.

The methodology employed a cultural approach, one specifically situated in teaching composition through literature. Lee (2007) puts it this way: "A cultural modeling approach would pair exemplars of . . . genres from students' everyday experiences with film, television, music, and oral traditions" (p. 40). Lee's research is with speakers of AAVE and the high school literature classroom, but what she promotes has relevance in the college composition setting, both for the AAVE-speaking students and the Chinese students in this example. Smitherman's (2000, p. 33) portrait of culture as "not just things, objects or material artefacts [but] more importantly . . . ways of thinking, behavioral patterns of conduct and language" is also instructive.

Smitherman continues by commending the work of ethnographers for reminding structural linguists that "language cannot be abstracted from the sociocultural context" (2000, p. 83). The real components of rhetorical power lie in the communicative art of persuasion. The makeup of the audience and its understanding of context is of critical value to the rhetor. Successful communication cannot take place without an understanding of this basic building block. The aim of composition is to have students who can perform communicative art.

According to Dillard (1972, p. 289), "In order for the teaching experience to be [properly] fitted to the [student's] own cultural background, it is quite important for the teacher to *know* [my emphasis] something about that background." For the AAVE-speaking student, as Lee (2007) points out, the use of cultural references from genres of art familiar to her are most helpful. For the Chinese students, an assignment for which they were required to transliterate an American cultural experience into a Chinese one served this purpose.

Because language is tied to intellectual (cognitive) organization of the environment, a system of mental representations and computations (Chomsky, 1988/2004), then giving students an opportunity to use a familiar environment to demonstrate their facility with English made for a much more engaging experience. Even though the assignment reversed the students' interpretation of everyday experiences, which posed a different problem from the one that they met in a canonical text, the result was the same.

The Chinese students were able to successfully bridge the gap of communicating an essentially Chinese experience through the transliteration of a scene from Salinger's *Catcher in the Rye*. The assignment required all students in the class, including the Chinese speakers, to rewrite a scene from the novel into a present-day scenario while retaining the literary elements of the textual passage. Working from a written description of the selected scene, the final presentation was to be visual, thereby demonstrating the ability to compose across mediums (written and oral).

The Chinese students excelled, choosing to revise one of the classic scenes: Holden Caufield's experiences in a New York night club. They placed him in a twenty-first-century Chinese nightclub. While the written portion of the assignment was at the novice level, the discussion of their visual presentation was superb. Because the context was one with which they were familiar, they were able to focus on the English language descriptions and not the text (that they created).

The result was a thoroughly enjoyable and informative PowerPoint presentation. Teacher and students alike were able to move from what Dillard (1972, p. 278) describes as the "confines of grading [in] search of the misspelled word, comma [splices] and sentence fragments"; away from what Smitherman (2000, p. 131) terms the quintessential response to poorly written argument papers—"correct your grammar and resubmit." We entered the realm of teacher innovation, devised to put more control for learning this thing called Standard English into the hands of those who speak it as an additional variety.

This example contrasts sharply with that of an urban institution where there was much more emphasis on strict conformity to the rhetorical moves of Standard English. How do instructors reach this goal with a student population whose speech community performs another variety of English, and whose fluency with the vagaries of Standard English is at the novice level at best? For the Chinese students, their success in the course did not depend on a level of mastery of SE. While the challenges of ESD speakers are not the primary challenge in the urban college composition classroom, there are practical ways to incorporate AAVE into the teaching of composition for these students by providing a basic understanding of the linguistic elements of the home language as contrasted with those of SE.

Logic and Black English

It is a shame that the logic of language—especially in the teaching of surface structural elements (grammar rules)—is not taught consistently in composition classes. As Chomsky (1988/2004, p. 128) reminds us, "a person's knowledge of [her] language is based on a system of rules and principles," even if the person can't articulate the rules. As indicated earlier, a baby learning to speak English of the standard variety may be heard to say *I goed* (someplace). She is not incorrect. Her construction is a result of learning that the past tense is created by adding *-ed.* Lee (2007) also chimes in, pointing out that "it is possible to reason ... in a so-called vernacular variety of a national language" (p. 85).

By way of illustration, let us visit another much-maligned feature of AAVE: its use of aspectual verb system rules applied to the verb *to be*. As a reminder: Aspect is a grammatical category that expresses how an action, event, or state, denoted by a verb, extends over time. Further distinctions can be made, for example, to distinguish states and ongoing actions (continuous and progressive aspects) from repetitive actions (habitual aspect).

Smitherman (2000) offers a reference for teaching this particular point of grammar. What is the difference between the sentences *The coffee be cold* and *The coffee cold*? In the first sentence, the speaker is relaying the fact that the coffee is always cold. In the second sentence, the coffee is cold at this moment. Speakers of SE would use the sentence *The coffee is cold* to express both actions. Comparison and contrast of the two varieties can lead to a robust discussion about not only tense formation, but also other stylistic features of both varieties—features such as cadence, rhythm, gestures, and all those other elusive, difficult-to-objectify elements that make up what is considered writing in a speaker's style (Smitherman, 2000).

Such discussions can highlight the contributions of AAVE to learning. Smitherman continues her argument by referencing that there is no essential linguistic difference between *dis heah* and *this here*, both of that are problematic for SE purists, but understood by speakers of all varieties. Chomsky would argue that the deep structure of both is the same. Lee (2007) has the final word on this model, stating that "reasoning ... is the most important task for teaching ... not only [for] simplistic syntax formulas for communicating ideas in Academic English [but] for learning to [code-switch]" (p. 85). And there you have the foundation for creating grammar standards, targets, and associated lesson plans from AAVE.

In the absence of like models, for teachers of freshman composition courses with class rosters primarily made up of AAVE speakers, adapting existing textbooks through cultural transliterations combined with creating off-the-cuff code-switches is in fact the central task of each day. Most commonly, teaching approaches in this setting rely on representing the SE code into examples transliterated into AAVE or, at the very least, given in the cultural context of AAVE. Teachers who are native speakers of AAVE switch back and forth on a daily basis, depending upon mood and audience. They are bi-dialectical (in case you haven't noticed, there have been a few code-switches in this chapter).

Another example from personal teaching experience serves as an illustration. In explaining vague pronoun referents, there is a conscious effort to include the comical and even stereotypical names of two girls—Shenaynay and LaQuisha—who go together to the corner store to buy potato chips and hot sauce, delicacies in da hood. "She also bought an orange pop." "Who is she?" the class is asked. Since *errybody* in the class can envision the scene, the only decoding that has to take place is determining the correct answer to the question. Now while this example may be a bit simplistic, it accurately depicts the inclusion of cultural reference points.

The relevance of cultural references has been introduced briefly. But a review is appropriate at this juncture. In her recommendations for furthering the cause of AAVE's place in academic settings, Smitherman (2000) reminds us that we don't typically teach cultural roles as part of current classroom curriculum. This deficiency is what allows the textbook publisher McGraw-Hill to release a high school geography text that referred to the Middle Passage as the route African "workers" took to reach America. Workers rather than slaves! The ensuing controversy stirred up lots of reactions, the most virulent of which came from Black people whose slave ancestors must have been turning in their graves.

The entire incident, however, has relevance—though in a negative sense—to the discussion of cultural data sets modeled by Lee (2007) and their effectiveness in understanding elements of language in a cultural context. What motive would cause someone to equate the status of a slave with that of a worker? And while the slavery experience is not part of a Black student's everyday experience, it certainly informs her interpretation of what she reads.

Cultural data sets, according to Lee (2007, p. 61), "provide students with support for making public and explicit the tacit knowledge they possess about how to make sense of a particular kind of problem [and to] provide them with a language to talk about [that problem]." Most importantly, Lee continues, cultural data sets "make connections between what [students] do [speak AAVE] and what they are expected to do [speak SE]" (p. 61). Imagine the language that might have been used to describe the problem with the textbook entry. What rhetorical processes of AAVE (exaggerated language and wordplay, for example) might have been employed?

Equally Yoking AAVE and SE

Personal experience has taught that Black instructors teaching college composition courses at an urban university understand that their personal use of AAVE is critical to knowledge transfer. While at White institutions AAVE usage is relegated to discussions with the relatively few people of color who are English majors and the even fewer faculty of color, for urban faculty, it is an essential tool of communication. Teachers are regularly called upon to translate rhetoric texts into AAVE in order to connect with their students—and sometimes even to understand a fine point of grammar themselves! Needing to do such translation daily and on the spot is taxing.

We must have AAVE transliterated textbooks that contrast AAVE with SE as a means of unpacking the underlying logic of both, and to facilitate learning the intricacies of the latter. Such texts exist at the high school and primary school levels—this was perhaps the most immediate takeaway from the Oakland decision. But are there examples of such for college-level composition courses? For if such texts are crucial in the K–12 classroom, how much more important they become for the first-year, urban, first-generation college student whose K–12 experience may have failed to value her home speech community, and most likely shortchanged her in the study of Standard English as well.

The continuing underfunding of schools in Black communities across the American landscape leaves Black students at all levels at a disadvantage when it comes to mastery of marketplace English. In fact, putting the issue into a historical perspective, Smitherman (2000) refers to the 1997 congressional hearing on Ebonics at which data was presented that tracked "the most critical basic skill—reading" of Black children: "At age nine [they] are 27 points behind in reading; at age 17, they are 37 points behind" (p. 119).

And yes, these data are from over twenty years ago. But we have to ask: Has the overall achievement levels of Black children *advanced*? Have there been *positive consequences* of No Child Left Behind, or the fast-growing charter school movement? Our children are passed along, entering college with major deficits and ill equipped to process academic English.

And so, we argue that Black English must become an additional lingua franca in the composition classroom to mitigate the struggles of writing. Jessica Whitney's (2005) argument that AAVE must be valued in the classroom can be extended to include the phrase *any* classroom, for, as she presents, "AAVE in the classroom is not about eradicating education about the English language," but about "building on home language to teach about Standard English" (p. 64).

How we define literacy—reading and writing—must take into consideration one's ability to read the world, to own a means of knowing—an ontological frame of reference. For students whose first English is AAVE, a Du Boisian double consciousness is required. And composition classes can address this need by incorporating code-switching as a matter of course. Thus, literacy for the speaker of Standard English as a second dialect becomes the ability to appropriately and correctly switch between AAVE and Standard English according to the dictates of audience and context.

One of the most important needs fulfilled by textbooks for adult speakers of AAVE enrolled in college-level composition courses is providing a standardized guide for instructors who are unfamiliar with AAVE. Non-AAVE-speaking teachers are in-classroom exemplars of the status quo for college Standard English. Their very presence can inhibit dialectal exchange while inadvertently reinforcing inferiority about AAVE. As Reed (1973) points out, and as many Black instructors know from experience, "if [the] teacher is Black, [the student] will most likely feel freer about [discussing ethnic characteristics of his language behavior]. If the teacher is white . . . the student [may] resent the teacher's calling attention to what he regards as an embarrassing deficiency" (p. 294).

Like Reed, Whitney (2005) has a rubric for incorporating AAVE in the classroom, although her approach comes from a K–12 teaching environment. As her article "Five Easy Pieces: Steps toward Incorporating AAVE into the Classroom" suggests, she has created a list of tools for accomplishing this task: Self-education of the teacher is ranked as step one. The critical nature of knowing the culture from which students emerge, coupled with more than a surface familiarity with AAVE, is a requisite. Step two—incorporation of multiculturalism into the classroom—is another strategy for easing the struggle of first-generation college students.

Whitney's list also includes creating a learning environment that values oral traditions and encourages code-switching. And yet, perhaps her most important step, and the one that is classroom user-friendly, is permitting students to, as Whitney puts it, "write like real writers" (p. 68). After all, isn't this type of performance a basic tenet of college introductory rhetoric courses? Whitney's fifth step emphasizes the audience and its role in shaping the composition. The audience of course is an integral side of the isosceles triangle that illustrates basic rhetorical considerations.

So how might a teacher incorporate this learning module into a classroom of AAVE speakers? Here is one example that we have used in an urban college's composition class. A typical assignment for the first week of class is to write an expository essay on that week's campus experience. We assigned two essays, each for a different audience: (1) the teacher and grader of fluency with Standard English, and (2) a favorite homie, BFF, or posse member. The results consistently revealed not only the inclusion of different experiences of interest (or presumed interest to each audience), but also a different use of grammar and word choice.

It is reasonable to expect a heavy use of AAVE in the essay targeted to friends, and to see attempts at SE usage in the essay meant for the teacher. Together, the class used these differences to begin the transliteration process, and in the process unpack Hurston's assertion that the greatest contribution of the Black man in America has been to the English language. Hurston gave credit well in advance of today's dominance of pop culture by Black stylistic language variations.

Again, like Reed (1973), Whitney (2005) also acknowledges the need to uncouple AAVE from thoughts of inferiority regarding communication patterns. However, she differs in approach. Whitney lobbies for "a learning environment that values diversity in experience, culture, and language" (p. 65)—in other words, incorporation of the social justice issues that play out in contemporary society and that are most certainly not absent from educational settings. More narrowly, however, the multiculturalism that is so useful as a teaching tool is not limited to racial and ethnic diversity. Cultural behaviors themselves can be used as examples for instruction in Standard English composition classes.

The mini-lesson on the logic of sentence/paragraph transitions, using a demonstration of the pivot move in basketball, was a case in point. This mini-lesson was inspired by Hurston's (1934/1994) essay and her illumination of the Negro's tendency to *think* in pictures. This is a major point both Reed and Whitney are making, one that can guide teacher preparation for AAVE speaking students—to master this so-called Standard English, one must *think*. As Jones (2014, n.p.) puts it, the relevance of using AAVE as a "bridge to teach AAVE-speaking children how to speak and write Standard American English" is obvious. This bridge needs to be extended to adult learners as well.

The references for this chapter became as partners on a personal dance card. A final and valuable partner, *Articulate while Black: Barack Obama, Language, and Race in the U.S.* (2012), coauthored by H. Samy Alim and Geneva Smitherman with a foreword by Michael Eric Dyson, was useful in organizing the content of this chapter. The colleague who recommended this text ain't nevah lied.

The text, which utilizes Barack Obama as the linchpin for a cogent discussion of language and race in the United States, is a wonderful read. But it also succinctly illustrates some of our points about the need for bi-dialectical texts for college composition courses. Smitherman of course is a master code-switcher, and Alim, her student, has not fallen far from the tree. Together they have crafted a text that presents the relevant issues in an entertaining and thought-provoking manner. The combination of current, hot-off-the-press topics speaks directly to the cultural contexts so important to the incorporation of AAVE in the college classroom. As Dyson (2012) points out in his foreword:

> Black speech is always much more than what things are said, but about how those things are said. And how those things are said involves, of course, the mechanics of grammar, the intonations, the pace, the cadence, and the flow of Black rhetoric, but it includes as well the political and social realities that weigh on the tongue. (p. xi)

Dyson's words and indeed the thesis of the Alim and Smitherman text speak a generally unspoken truth and relate directly to Smitherman's (2000) connections between language and social capital. She writes that "language is integral to the African American struggle for empowerment . . . it plays a dominant role in the formation of ideology, consciousness, and class relations" (p. 43). In other words, language is a construction of reality from the perspective of sociolinguistics.

Smitherman continues, "language power is a function not of one's dialect [or variety], but of larger linguistic structures skillfully and effectively employed" (p. 121). Proper use of language, any language, is inextricably tied to one's ability to think, to communicate effectively, and to operate successfully in different environments. These skills are layered within what Chomsky identifies as language's deep structure, and AAVE has those structures. Their presence is what makes Hurston's claim about characteristics of our speech so thought-provoking and right on.

We argue for the equal yoking of AAVE with SE in our classrooms, for the betterment of Black students, but also for the betterment of society as a whole. Transliterations of SE to AAVE can be applied directly to create lessons that contrast and compare the two varieties. Assessments can then be designed that measure the student's ability to predict that the construction is appropriate and similar in meaning. To achieve the mastery in all this is the goal. Achieving mastery empowers the student in a practical way—she becomes more skilled at the tango of language usage. Here's hoping the dance card will be filled with partners for this tango . . . or line dance . . . or Chicago steppin'.

Chapter 4

Pedagogical Techniques for Teaching AAVE Speakers

One major concern reported by faculty who teach linguistically diverse students is that they either do not have the appropriate training to address the literacy skills their students bring to the classroom, or they do not have the resources to do so (C. A. Williams, 2014). To address this concern, this chapter reviews the theoretical contributions of Lisa Delpit and James Paul Gee, provides sample lessons and activities, and offers a sample syllabus that can be used to develop a course on teaching AAVE speakers.

The activities included in this chapter come from a course that was developed to examine language, culture, and power. This course introduces students to linguistics, but focuses primarily on reading contexts and looking at the ways language and the culture of power align. Throughout the course, students are required to analyze discourse and make connections between language in use (speaking and listening to language in various contexts) and language expectations (considering the ways context establishes discourse communities and expectations).

THEORETICAL UNDERPINNINGS

Both Delpit (1995a, 1995b, 2002) and Gee (1989a, 1989b, 1998, 1999, 2001) explore literacy through a sociocultural lens and give a great deal of consideration to the ways language and power are linked and play out in our day-to-day lives. What interested us in our discussion of their work was the way Delpit confronts her concerns with Gee's approach. In her article, "The Politics of Teaching Literate Discourse," Delpit (1995a) explicitly addresses her concerns with Gee's (1989a) arguments for an apprentice approach to teaching minorities mainstream discourse. Delpit (1995a) states,

> There are two aspects of Gee's arguments which I find problematic. First is Gee's notion that people who have not been born into dominant discourses will find it exceedingly difficult, if not impossible, to acquire such a discourse. He argues strongly that discourses cannot be "overtly" taught, particularly in a classroom, but can only be acquired by enculturation in the home or by "apprenticeship" into social practice. The second argument of Gee's work that I find troubling suggests that an individual who is born into one discourse with one set of values may experience major conflicts when attempting to acquire another discourse with another set of values. (pp. 546–547)

Delpit (1995a) sees the apprentice approach as relying too heavily on the idea that if teachers model discourse, students will automatically try to replicate what they see their teachers doing. Her concern is that the apprentice model is too implicit. As Gee (1989a, 1989b) states, mainstream discourse is the language of the middle class, and is replicated in other mainstream environments.

> Delpit (1995b) addresses the differences in the ways that cultures use language with the following example:
> Other researchers have identified differences in middle-class and working-class speech in children. . . . Middle-class parents are likely to give the directive to a child to take his bath as, "Isn't it time for your bath?" By contrast, a black mother, in whose house I was recently a guest, said to her eight-year-old son, "Boy, get your rusty behind in that bathtub." (p. 34)

In Delpit's example, she highlights the ways language is used differently in these two spaces. Delpit (1995b) references Heath's work (not by specific year) in her explanation of this example by saying, "Consequently, as Heath suggests, upon entering school the child from such a family may not understand the indirect statement of the teacher as a direct command" (p. 34). According to Delpit (1995a, 1995b, 2002), it is socially unjust not to require students to use the codes that will be used by society to judge them and exclude them. However, as will be discussed later in this chapter, Delpit does not suggest that one code has to be sacrificed in order for the other code to be acquired.

Gee (1989a, 1989b, 1998, 2001, 2004, 2007, 2011) expands the idea of literacy as being more than a person's ability to display basic skills in reading and writing; he states that any useful definition of literacy must include one's ability to demonstrate the right type of reading, writing, and speaking based on context. In our classroom activities, we sought to intentionally provide opportunities for students to practice identifying context, which tends to be the major concern when enacting context-specific discourse.

It is not that students are unaware that certain spaces expect specific ways of reading, writing, and speaking; it is that they have a difficult time identifying those spaces, or lack experience in those spaces. As a result, they default to a way of reading, writing, and speaking that might not match the context but has resulted in success in other situations. It is this understanding that led us to develop classroom activities that build schema through using examples that uncover context-specific ways of carrying out day-to-day communicative tasks, such as asking for a pen. We recognize that these instances are difficult to create or identify in "real time," so our activities allow students to employ them in a variety of ways and spaces.

Gee's (1989a) notion of literacy includes the idea that context matters, and he argues that to be literate in one context may not equate to being literate in another context. When reflecting on our students, we realize that they have lived and continue to live full lives outside of school, and they use literacy in nuanced ways that render them successful. To not acknowledge and help our students remember their successes would situate us in savior positions, which is a space we are not interested in occupying. Gee (1989a) provides the following example of the complexities of context-specific literacy:

> It is a truism that a person can know perfectly good grammar of a language and not know how to use that language. If I enter my neighborhood bar and say to my tattooed drinking buddy, as I sit down, "May I have a match please?," my grammar is perfect, but what I have said is wrong nonetheless. It is not just *how* you say it, but what you *are* and *do* when you say it. If I enter my neighborhood bar and say to my drinking buddy, as I sit down, "Gimme a match, wouldya?," while placing a napkin on the bar stool to avoid getting my newly pressed designer jeans dirty, I have said the right thing, but my "saying-doing" combination is nonetheless all wrong. (p. 525)

To teach a person how to apply the "right" type of literacy based on context, Gee (1989a, 1989b) offered apprenticeships or enculturation as the best method of instruction for groups who have been socialized outside of mainstream—or as he calls it, discourse, contexts. Delpit (1995a, 1995b, 2002) might point out that although Gee's (1989a) idea of speaking and acting is a connected activity, when looking at his example of bar culture, it is based on stereotypical ideas.

Gee's (1989a) example leaves out mention of culture, which is a part of language use. Is this a White bar? Is this a sports bar? All of these things determine the "rightness" or "wrongness" of his actions. In addition, schema matters when determining the "right" language to use. For example, as African American women, in our experience, it would not be far-fetched to enter a local bar or lounge in an urban neighborhood and request a match by saying, "May I have a match please?" We do recognize that at the time of Gee's (1989a) example, tattoos may not have been as common and carried a different social stigma, but this lends itself to our earlier discussion about the ways perceptions and experiences are shaped.

In short, Delpit (1995a, 1995b, 2002) calls for more explicit instruction, whereas Gee (1989a, 1989b, 1998, 1999, 2001) calls for apprenticeships and more implicit instruction. Ladson-Billings (1994, 1995, 2002, 2005) and Young (2004) share similar ideas with Delpit concerning how teachers might approach teaching mainstream literacy expectations. Our perspectives are aligned to a more explicit approach as well.

The research exploring literacy, language, and discourse argues that for one to master the dominant discourse, he or she must sacrifice his or her own discourse, which is connected to his or her identity (Gee, 1989a, 1989b, 2001). Delpit (1995a) states, "Acquiring the ability to function in a dominant discourse need not mean that one must reject one's home identity and values, for discourses are not static, but are shaped, however reluctantly, by those who participate within them and by the form of their participation" (p. 552).

Some linguists argue that the mechanical and grammatical features of SE are superficial features. Gee (1989a) argues that these features are often used to "test" if a student is a member of a particular discourse community. Delpit (1995a) states that not requiring students to show competency in these "superficial features" does the exact opposite of the goal; rather, it oppresses these students.

Delpit (1995a), through discussion with colleagues who had successfully acquired a discourse that they were not born with, identifies the following as characteristics of teachers who have helped students successfully acquire dominant discourses:

1. "Teachers successfully taught what Gee calls the 'superficial features' of middle-class discourse-grammar, style, mechanics—features that Gee claims are particularly resistant to classroom instruction" (p. 549).
2. "Teachers insisted that students be able to speak and write eloquently, maintain neatness, think carefully, exude character, and conduct themselves with decorum" (p. 549).
3. As reflected by one of her colleagues, teachers "held visions of us that we could not imagine for ourselves. They were determined that, despite all odds, we would achieve" (p. 549).

What these characteristics have in common are not just the teacher explicitly teaching students about language and grammar, but the teacher believing that success for these students is possible and feeling responsible for their journey.

The difference between the explicit approach that Delpit (1995a) discusses and the apprenticeship that Gee (1989a) offers is that Gee (1989a) says that an apprenticeship must be supported by interaction with people who have already mastered the discourse, which means they may be operating inside of the margin. Delpit (1995a) points out that many of the teachers who supported their students' successful acquisition of the discourse "were denied entry into the larger White world" (p. 549). Therefore, they were teaching from the margins, trying to help their students get in. They took responsibility for their students' life successes. According to Du Bois (1903/1994), they were teaching students double-consciousness. They were teaching them that they do not have to believe all of the views and ideas of the mainstream in order to acquire the mainstream way of communicating and being in the mainstream world. Their students just had to understand that the differences exist, and how to negotiate those differences while maintaining their cultural identities.

What follows are examples of instructional materials that demonstrate how much of the content explored in this book "looks" in practice. The reality is that doing the work to shape or sharpen students' literacy skills does not *have* to be a daunting task, and opportunities to do so must be instructional and nonjudgmental. This work is already sensitive, and faculty who take on the responsibility of doing this work must do so with compassion and the realization that the social skills that students bring to the teaching and learning environment are rooted in culture and beliefs that have generally served them well up until this point.

Instead of asking students to completely remove their ways of knowing and communicating, we are encouraging students to add to that toolkit. The following materials have been used in the postsecondary classroom and have been adapted to professional development activities for postsecondary faculty.

STRUCTURE OF ACTIVITIES

The activities are presented in a way that borrows from Bloom's taxonomy. Instead of a bottom-up approach that places *identify* at the bottom, it places it at the top as a starting point. Another concern faculty have around addressing students' social literacy skills is that, often, the tension between students' home literacies and what is expected in academic contexts is difficult to pinpoint and develop. These activities are organized from the stance that first, students must be able to identify the social literacy skills that they bring to academic settings and those skills expected of academic settings.

Often, instructors take for granted what students know and understand about the world and the fluid nature of expectations. By engaging students in activities that help them identify what they do and then leading them through activities that uncover what is expected, students are able to make the necessary connections and adjustments. Furthermore, these activities provide students with opportunities to practice making connections before they are in the heat of the moment, so to speak.

Activity Type: Identify

Activity #1: Teaching Language Use and Choices

Directions: As we discussed, there are many ways to say something, and how we decide to say something may be based on the person/people we are talking to and the environment we are in. Use the following chart to help you see the difference between how we talk and write in different situations and for different purposes.

Part I: Setting the Context

1. Describe the way you communicate at home.
   When Speaking   *When Writing*

2. Describe the way you communicate at school.
   When Speaking   *When Writing*

3. Describe the way you communicate at work.
   When Speaking   *When Writing*

Part II: Language in Practice

Prompt A: You want to ask to use a book. In the spaces provided, write out how you would ask someone to use a book in the three provided environments (home, school, work). Try not to give this a lot of thought.
   At Home   *At School*   *At Work*

Prompt B: Now you want to leave someone a written note asking to use a book. In the spaces provided, write a brief note asking someone to use a book

in the three provided environments (home, school, work). Try not to give this a lot of thought.
At Home   *At School*   *At Work*

Prompt C: You want to ask if a seat is available. In the spaces provided, write out how you would ask someone if a seat is available in the three provided environments (home, school, work). Try not to give this a lot of thought.
At Home   *At School*   *At Work*

Prompt D: Now you want to give someone a written note asking if a seat is available. In the spaces provided, write a brief note asking someone if a seat is available in the three provided environments (home, school, work). Try not to give this a lot of thought.
At Home   *At School*   *At Work*

Prompt E: You want to ask for permission to enter a room. In the spaces provided, write out how you would ask someone to enter a room in the three provided environments (home, school, work). Try not to give this a lot of thought.
At Home   *At School*   *At Work*

Part III: Reflection

At this point, take a look at the responses you provided for parts I–II. In the space below, reflect on any differences you notice based on context. Where do you think you were introduced to communicating in each context? Do you think there is any overlap? Also, note any additional thoughts about the activity.

Rationale

Activity #1 serves as an entry point into starting the discussion around how and why context matters. Specifically, allowing students to write out how they would respond to each prompt, verbally and in writing, while considering the environment in which the activity is taking place allows them to examine their ways of communicating and their understanding of the expectations of the particular spaces outside of the moment. This activity requires a high level of reflection before and after the activity. It provides them with an artifact that requires reflection before completing.

We are trying to get our students to be more reflective before speaking and writing. Also, it provides the instructor with insight into how students perceive each environment, and a point to start the discussion around the social expectations of each environment. Although this activity is presented as an entry point, instructors can provide them to students in the order they see fit.

Activity Type: Observe

Activity #2: Observation Discourse Map

Directions: For this activity, you must go to an event or a place where people who share similar characteristics (age, ethnicity, culture, gender, students, etc.) are gathered. This can be a formal event or a trip to the cafeteria at school. At this event or place, you should (1) identify the characteristics that they all share, (2) observe their actions, and (3) listen to how they communicate. Now, pay attention to your responses to items 1–3. Begin to connect how they use language and communication to become recognized as a member of that particular community. Use the diagram to identify the discourse strands you observe. An example has been provided to help get you started.

Figure 4.1 provides an example of an observation discourse map completed during a visit to a university cafeteria. Items inside the circle represent the recognition work (Gee, 2011) that people do to be recognized as members of a particular community. The outer rectangles represent the various characteristics or communities represented in a particular space. These can represent a single person or a group of people, but either way the participants are doing some work, either consciously or unconsciously, to represent the group, act out an identity, or announce themselves as a member of the larger group.

It is important that students understand that they hold membership in multiple communities, and that each community has a specific set of characteristics; whether they realize it or not, they either represent themselves as a member or an imposter when they are in that community setting. Figure 4.2 is an example of the actual graphic that would be provided to students to complete.

Rationale

According to Gee (1989a), a person's ability to use discourse fluently announces him or her as a member of an environment or as one who is not fluent. Students typically take on the role of apprentices when instructors

Figure 4.1. Example of an observation discourse map.

act as mentors (Gee, 2001). There are multiple ways in which people recognize others that Gee (2011) discusses in his work. Delpit (1995a) provides codes of power as one way that people identify themselves as members of a group. According to Gee (2011), the issue is a problem of "recognition and being recognized" (p. 24). This activity allows students to make some observations about how language is being used in multiple ways and for various purposes.

Activity Type: Apply

Activity #3: Discourse Identification Sheet

Directions: For this activity, you must either attend or watch a formal event. This can range from a seminar or lecture held about a particular topic, or you can watch a political event on television. You are observing a single person who has been selected to speak to an audience. Address the provided questions related to the speaker only.

    Event:_____ Purpose:_____

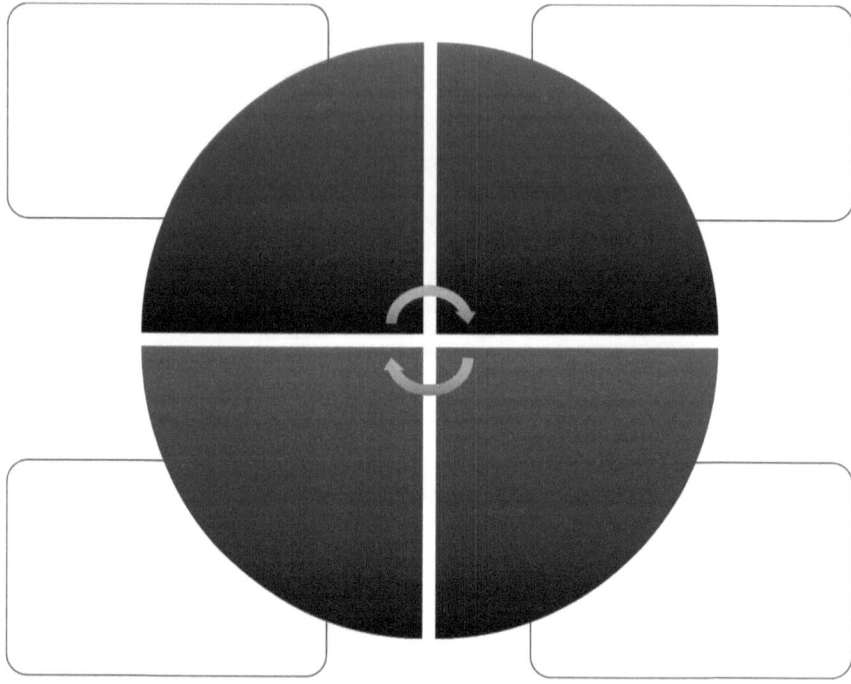

Figure 4.2. Discourse map template.

1. What did you know about the speaker before the observation?
2. What assumptions did you make about the speaker based on his or her speaking?
3. What discourse strand(s) does the speaker use?
4. What recognition work does the speaker do during the event? (This is not limited to language.)
5. How does the speaker use language to identify with the audience?
6. How does the speaker include certain groups of people through language?
7. How does the speaker exclude certain groups of people through language?
8. How did the speaker's language establish and maintain the purpose of the event?
9. How did the speaker negotiate language (standard and social)?
10. Provide additional comments or observations.

Rationale

Students tend to be either observers or receivers of information, more than givers. To that end, it is important that they are able to identify not only their own language use, but also the language use of others. This activity allows them to apply what they did in Activity #1, where they had to identify their own language use, and in Activity #2, where they had to observe the language use of others, to an analysis of a speaker who is intentionally and strategically using language, or discourse, to advance his or her particular purpose.

SAMPLE COURSE SYLLABUS INFORMATION

As we discussed throughout this text, many college faculty have never received teacher preparation training. In some graduate programs, graduate students are only required to complete training if they serve as teaching assistants. To better prepare college faculty, some graduate programs are developing courses that include similar components to those that would be found in a K–12 teaching methods course. We provide here a sample syllabus of such a course. This course was developed at a predominantly Black institution (PBI) to better prepare English majors who have an interest in teaching, at both the secondary and postsecondary level.

Course Description

Study and practice of Standard American English, code-switching, and rhetorical and dialectical theory, with a heavy emphasis on oral language practice. This class will approach literacy as a cultural and social practice. The work of James Gee, Lisa Delpit, Gloria Ladson-Billings, Victoria Purcell-Gates, and others will be explored. Students will begin to develop an understanding of code-switching, code-meshing, and other strategies used to help negotiate vernacular use and the language of the marketplace.

Required Textbooks

Lindquist, J., & Seitz, D. (2008). *The elements of literacy.* New York, NY: Longman.
Perry, T., & Delpit, L. (1998). *The real Ebonics debate.* Boston, MA: Beacon.

Student Outcomes

At the conclusion of the class, students will be able to perform the following:

1. Write and speak using standard American English.
2. Understand and be able to articulate the work of literacy scholars and their theoretical frameworks.
3. Analyze dialect use in writing and speaking, integrating the written work of others and listening to the speech patterns of others.
4. Understand literacy as a social and cultural practice.
5. Develop instructional materials for linguistically diverse students.

Professional Standards

All assignments follow the standards put forth by the following:

- Council for the Accreditation of Educator Preparation (CAEP)
- Specialized Professional Association and Specialized Accrediting Organization (SPA/SAO)
- National Council for Teachers of English (NCTE)

Assessment: LiveText is *required* for this course.
Weekly reflection papers = 10 pts each
Five-week assessments = 20 pts each
In-class writing activities = 5 pts each
Oral assessment = 50 pts each

Course Schedule

For our class readings, candidates are required to bring three discussion questions related to the reading material for the evening to each class meeting. The questions may be collected. Please note, not all in-class activities and quizzes are listed in the following outline. Although students are not given points for simply attending class, there may be multiple opportunities to earn points when present in class. If a student is not in class, the student misses the opportunity to earn the points.

BIBLIOGRAPHY OF ADDITIONAL COURSE READINGS

Gee, J. P., & Green, J. (1998). Discourse analysis, learning, and social practice: A methodological study. *Review of Research in Education, 23,* 119–169.

Heath, S. B. (1983). *Ways with words: Language, life and work in communities and classrooms.* New York, NY: Cambridge University Press.

Table 4.1: Course Schedule

Date	Due This Week	Class Activity	When You Leave	Text
Week 1		Course introduction Syllabus overview	Chapter 1	Lindquist & Seitz (2008)
Week 2	Chapter 1 Reflection paper	Literacy: More than reading and writing Discussion of chapter 1	Chapter 2	Lindquist & Seitz (2008)
Week 3	Chapter 2 Reflection paper	Literacy and the mind Discussion of chapter 2 Literacy practice	Chapter 3 Ways with Words Analyzing Literacy Practice	Lindquist & Seitz (2008); Heath (1983, 1989); Purcell-Gates (2002)
Week 4	Chapter 3 Reflection paper	Literacy and culture Discussion of chapter 3	Chapter 4	Lindquist & Seitz (2008)
Week 5	Chapter 4 Reflection paper	Five-week assessment Literacy and class Discussion of chapter 4	See course shell for additional readings	
Week 6	New literacy studies	A critical discussion of the new literacy studies	Street Critical Discussion of New Literacy Studies	Street (1984, 1995, 2003); Stephens (2011)
Week 7	Discourse analysis	An introduction to discourse analysis	Discourse Analysis, Learning, and Social Practice	Gee & Green (1998)

Date	Due This Week	Class Activity	When You Leave ...	Text
Week 8	Critical reader response covering both readings	The Ebonics debate	Introduction Cultural Modeling Students' Right to Their Own Language	Perry & Delpit (1998); Lee (1995); Smitherman (1995)
Week 9	Critical reader response	What is Ebonics?	Chapter 2	Perry & Delpit (1998)
Week 10		Five-week assessment	Chapter 3	Perry & Delpit (1998)
Week 11	Critical reader response	Quiz Classroom implications	Chapter 4 *King v. Ann Arbor*	Perry & Delpit (1998); William and Mary Law Review (1979)
Week 12	Personal essay: Exploring your relationship with language	Review the Oakland resolution and *King v. Ann Arbor*	Chapter 5	Perry & Delpit (1998)
Week 13		Field observations		
Week 14	Field notes	Discuss field observations Emerging questions/thoughts/ideas	Review all course readings	
Week 15		Final exam		

———. (1989). Oral and literate traditions among Black Americans living in poverty. *American Psychologist, 44*(2), 367–373.
Lee, C. (1995). A culturally based cognitive apprenticeship: Teaching African American high school students skills in literacy interpretation. *Reading Research Quarterly, 33*(4), 608–630.
Martin Luther King Jr., Etc. v. Ann Arbor Sch. Dist., 473 F. Supp. 1371 (E.D. Mich. 1979).
Purcell-Gates, V. (2002). ". . . As soon as she opened her mouth!": Issues of language, literacy, and power. In L. Delpit (Ed.), *The skin that we speak: Thoughts on language and culture in the classroom* (pp. 121–144). New York, NY: New York Press.
Smitherman, G. (1995). "Students' right to their own language": A retrospective. *English Journal, 84*(1), 21–27.
Stevens, L. P. (2011). Locating the role of the critical discourse analyst. In R. Rogers (Ed.), *Critical discourse analysis in educational settings* (2nd ed.). New York, NY: Routledge.
Street, B. V. (1984). *Literacy in theory and practice.* New York, NY: Cambridge University Press.
———. (1995). *Social literacies: Critical approaches to literacy in development, ethnography and education.* London, UK: Longman.
———. (2003). What's "new" in new literacy studies? Critical approaches to literacy in theory and practice. *Current Issues in Comparative Education, 5*(2), 77–91.

The readings reflected in the sample syllabus are not exhaustive, and surely can and must be expanded to include a range of discussion on the issue of ways to address teaching speakers of AAVE. The goal of this type of course is to introduce students to the theory and discussions around AAVE. This course is also a theory-to-practice type course, in that students are required to observe language in use in various contexts for the purpose of applying the theory from the readings to produce reflective writing. It is our hope that this type of course allows students to not only identify language variations in use by others, but reflect on how language variations operate in their own lives.

Assessments and Activities Related to the Sample Syllabus

The following assessments and activities are related to those reflected in the sample syllabus. Again, these assessments and activities are starting points for the ways in which students' knowledge and understanding about AAVE can be examined. These assessments and activities require students to actually demonstrate their understanding of course readings and their ability to analyze the major ideas in writing. These activities are designed to be reflective in nature.

Five-Week Assessment

Directions: Answer the following questions using complete sentences in Standard English.

1. What does Scribner mean by literacy as power?

2. According to Socrates, "This discovery of yours will create forgetfulness in the learners' souls, because they will not use their memories; they will trust to the external written characters and not remember of themselves. They will appear to be omniscient and will generally know nothing" (as cited in Lindquist & Seitz, 2009, p. 23). This is a two-part question:

    a. What is "this discovery of yours" (p. 23)?

    b. What does Socrates mean when he states, "They will appear to be omniscient and will generally know nothing" (p. 23)?

3. What is the claim of the "Great Divide" theorist?

4. Define literacy practices.

5. Define literacy event and who studied this concept.

6. Both Trackton and Roadville used storytelling; how did they use it differently?

7. Define communicative competence.

8. What is the difference between literacy skills and literacy behaviors?

Ten-Week Assessment: Discourse Analysis

This assignment should follow APA, 6th edition, format. You are expected to use outside sources to support your claims. This essay should be at least four pages of text in length.

Thus far, we have explored theory in the area of literacy. Specifically, we have explored literacy as a social practice and its implications for the mind, culture, and class. Tonight, many will tune in to the first of three presidential debates. Candidates will address issues that are considered public concerns. Both candidates will use literacy to reach a variety of viewers. They will strategically use words, body language, and other tactics (implicit or explicit) to connect with watchers. They will use intonation to communicate their messages, and they will need their language to reach across class, gender, race, culture, religion, and other indicators of diversity.

Your job is to analyze their discourse. Read James Gee's chapter (handout) to help you complete the discourse analysis. Also, re-read chapter 4 in the Lindquist and Seitz text. Specifically, focus on Gee's identity kit. What tools are in each candidate's identity kit? How do they use the tools to identify with viewers? Provide specific examples (and quotes) of the following literacy concepts:

- Mobility
- Gatekeeping
- Cultural capital
- Critical literacy

Our classroom activities were developed to provide scaffolded opportunities for students to practice various discourses. We want our students to see how they can manage their place in various discourse communities without sacrificing their identities. The hope is that students will see this task as achievable, and can use these activities as schema-building and activating points in future situations.

Chapter 5

What We Learned and What We Learnt

WHAT WE LEARNED

The imperative for a more culturally relevant and culturally sustaining and nuanced approach to teaching composition in urban colleges and universities is spawned by personal experiences, and not just those of first-generation college students whose struggles have inspired this text. It is also as a result of the microaggressions encountered by those of us who have multiple degrees, have academic positions at those same colleges and universities, and speak the King's English in a nearly perfect manner. For no one speaks collegiate English perfectly—witness the ongoing debate about the singular use of the plural pronoun *they*.

These instances of "my, you speak so well" or even "you sound White," an ultimate epithet used by us against us, contribute to a pervasive sense of linguistic inferiority among people of color in general and college students in particular. Even the aforementioned cadre of academically prepared professionals and educators are surely tired of asserting the validity of Black English when in the company of others. And unfortunately, some of us continue to dismiss any discussions about the utility of Black English as being divisive and nonprofessional—the Ebonics failure reprised in the twenty-first century.

The history of American English shows us that various dialects developed over time, and as John Baugh (2000) points out, a feeling of "linguistic liberation" and "gotcha" moments are invoked when we encounter educated Whites using *y'all*. Imagine then a similar sense of validation that can be experienced by Black students encountering teachers who also speak *their* language. Such a reality, coupled with texts that mirror the reality, can and does have a profound effect of the efficacy of student mastery and achievement.

But even when we *catch* them, we are not really catching them because the long-term implications for their use of *y'all* are not the same as when they catch us. When they catch us, they make assumptions about our lives in devaluing ways that seek to delegitimize our academic and professional success or achievements. It is similar to the *Saturday Night Live* skit titled *The Day Beyoncé Turned Black*, after the release of the "Formation" video. In the skit, White folks are seen reacting in terror at the idea that Beyoncé is actually Black and is concerned with issues that impact the Black community. They had accepted her, right? Why would she want to still associate with Blackness when she could be one of them? It was as if she had betrayed them in some way. It left us to question whether they were more outraged about her perceived antipolice messages or her explicit alignment with Black issues such as #BlackLivesMatter and, by extension, her communication of her Blackness and pride in everything associated with it.

There is also a twinge of classism in this disconnect between the teaching of college-level English and students whose primary spoken word is Black English. It is important to remember that public education—that is, education for the masses—was not the initial intent of early American institutions of higher learning. Access to colleges and universities was initially only available to the wealthy and served to maintain, and in many instances exacerbate, the gap separating the upper classes—in today's parlance the 1 percent—from the economically poor. So, one could argue that education is simply doing what education was meant to do in the first place.

The intention to maintain an ever-widening gap is exemplified by the assumption that the cultural context of White writers is the norm, even when their content explores historical times that are significant to Black people. The language of Horace Mann's Report No. 12 of the Massachusetts Board of Education, written in 1848, while potentially helpful in developing and evaluating contemporary educational practices, is beyond the reach of most of the Black English speech community today. It certainly can be problematic to the understanding and critique by first-generation urban college students.

The current over-reliance on achievement tests, which are patently biased both linguistically and culturally (Dillard, 1972) against speakers of Black English, is a major tool in the war to preserve achievement disparities. So, what can be done? A review of the strategies proposed by some of the scholars cited in this text offers solutions and hope. Dillard (1972) offers the format of initial studies of American Indian education as a reference point, noting "he would be taught standard English in the dialect most advantageous to him—as a second, alternate system" (pp. 270–71).

This observation is tied to Dillard's discussion of how acquisition of a variety of English works and the effect biases can have on one's ability to successfully master an additional dialect. Facility with language requires an internalization of rules that renders the need to stop and think about those rules as an indicator of failure: "If you have to stop and think [about how to transliterate], it's too late" (Dillard, 1972, p. 269). You are not yet fluent. Dillard continues with an essential understanding, the pejorative descriptor notwithstanding: "when doing their thing [speaking their variety of English], *ghetto* children are quite efficient" (1972, p. 274). It is from here where we can build their culturally sustaining capacity and argue that not knowing the rules to a new game does not mean that one lacks the ability to learn the rules and to be quite successful.

And yet this efficiency with their own mother tongue is dismissed by teachers who are too quick to profile them as uneducable. There is a validity to the reality of separation of Black students by means of their language usage. Teachers must exhibit an interest and curiosity about the words they use and the constructions they form. Dillard (1972) concludes that "the educational system [must] come to terms with the English the students [currently] speak" (p. 289). The cultural mismatch between reading materials and AAVE can be mitigated by substitutions that are akin to Lee's example of cultural data sets: "carefully [curated], culturally unbiased texts" (Dillard, 1972, p. 31) and their twenty-first-century counterparts—spoken word elegies and soliloquies.

John Baugh (2000) espouses an approach that also raises the specter of linguistic prejudice. In support of his point, Baugh offers the testimony of Supreme Court Justice Clarence Thomas during his confirmation hearings. Thomas is a native of Pin Point, Georgia, a rural community founded by freed slaves, located just outside Savannah and populated by Gullah speakers. In his testimony, Thomas relayed why his undergraduate major was English, indicating he had been advised to do so "because he spoke a foreign language" (Baugh, 2000, p. 114). But Thomas's language was not foreign at all; it was just foreign to those who passed judgement on him and others who spoke his language.

Rickford and Rickford (2000) introduce a specific classroom-based strategy, calling for reading lessons and activities that occur first in the native variety (AAVE), followed by a switch to SE. Lee (2007) underscores this point by identifying a fundamental problem of teaching: what to do after a student has answered a question in vernacular. Her solution? Reconfigure the answer in academic English, absent any negative assessment of the student's own language. Lee (2000) also advocates for strong opposition to the rising tendency of partisan politics to "selectively appropriate areas of educational research" (p. 179) and then mandate curriculum changes based on results. The decisions to cease teaching civics, phonetics, and cursive writing come to mind. But it is Smitherman (1994/2000, 2000) who offers the most comprehensive plan of those scholars, detailing a five-step action program.

First and foremost, Smitherman points to the need for an examination of lifestyles—the culture of the students and teachers. This step parallels Lee's cultural modeling approach for students—the inclusion of materials that are reflective of them. The next two planks in Smitherman's platform emphasize reading and oral work. Our earlier discussion on reading, again of materials that are culturally reflective of students, can be augmented by creative forays into oral presentations, cyphers, or alternating turns of spoken word. Smitherman specifically mentions improvisational drama, panel discussions, debates, and short speeches. And perhaps there is a need for the development of a postsecondary version of Flocabulary, the library of songs, videos, and activities for K–12 online learning of vocabulary.

More specifically adaptable to the urban college composition class is Smitherman's call for intensive study of language and culture. She calls our attention to the need for students "to achieve a broader understanding of the intricate connection between one's language and [their] cultural experience" (Smitherman, 2000, p. 120). But she also shines a light on the elephant in the room—the culture of teachers. She refers to the actual fact that "most English professors are trained in literature and have insufficient knowledge about language and language diversity" (Smitherman, 2000, 128).

Such a state of affairs results in the promotion of myths and biases about AAVE, coupled with a sadly undervalued understanding of not only "the psycho-cultural processes that guide the word selection by speakers of AAVE" but also comprehension on the part of teachers of "what the users use of [certain] words mean" (Smitherman, 2000, p. 61). But there is also a devaluing of AAVE's predominant rhetorical features, for example, spontaneity and the practice of call and response, which as Lee (2007) describes are indicators of student engagement and not intentionally disruptive behavior.

The corrective suggested by Smitherman is twofold: "in-service programs and workshops" (2000, p. 129), a model she alludes to as a successful tactic in providing knowledge about STEM. She also recognizes that whypipo don't have to learn AAVE but that "maybe teachers in urban settings should be required" (Smitherman, 2000, p. 80). This observation by Smitherman recalls a study cited by Dillard (1972) and conducted by William Alexander Stewart (1930–2002) while Stewart was on the faculty of Teachers College, Columbia University. According to Dillard, Stewart, known primarily for his work in AAVE, would turn the tables on teachers:

> Thus the linguist-teacher would give the cue sentence *He sick* and demand "Negative!". The accurate response would be *He ain't sick*. To the cue sentence *He be sick* the correct negative response is *He don't be sick*. Or [the

linguist-teacher] will demand the co-occurrent adverbial expression *all the time*; the only grammatical usage in Non-Standard dialect is *He be sick all the time*. With *right now*, on the other hand, the grammar demands *He sick right now*. *He sick all the time* and *He be sick right now* are unacceptable . . . grammatically incorrect in Black English. The aim of this kind of drill is to instill in the teacher not only respect for the language of the Black child, but also the knowledge—internalized, not just intellectualized—that there is a structure to the dialect, that one does not automatically produce a Negro [*sic*] Non-Standard English by simply breaking grammatical rules of standard English. Even more important, it aims to convey to the teacher the feelings of a student who finds he must use a language system superficially similar to but fundamentally different from the one he normally produces [or] his automatic responses may be subject to condemnation. (1972, p. 271)

Requiring reverse translations seems like an appropriate strategy to drive home the truth that Black English has grammatical rules. The work of developing such translation activities will require the involvement of AAVE-fluent rhetoricians and linguists.

Smitherman's fifth and final point focuses on policy, content, message, and the development of critical thinking. Teaching moments must focus on "the acquisition of those tools essential for thinking through a situation and making decisions" (Smitherman, 2000, p. 131). AAVE-speaking students need to understand the rules of SE in order to combat what Nikki Giovanni (1971) says is the "reason we always lose, not only 'cause we don't know the rules, but it ain't even our game" (Smitherman, 2000, p. 58). AAVE speakers come the arena prepared to play basketball, only to discover that it is an indoor tennis match.

And so Smitherman, in a simple example of combining SE and AAVE, names a primary need: "What we been needin is teachers with the proper attitudinal orientation who can distinguish actual reading problems from mere dialect differences" (2000, p. 58). Her point harkens back to Chomsky's deep and surface structure exegesis.

WHAT WE LEARNT

What we learnt is that when given support, our students, who primarily speak AAVE, can excel in mainstream spaces where SE is the expected style of communication in both writing and speaking. Instead of assuming that AAVE would be a barrier to our students' success, we made strategic instructional choices that would allow them to see how speaking AAVE has provided them with the intellectual flexibility to sustain their culturally connected way of communicating while adding to their literacy toolkit. To do this work can be intellectually and emotionally laborious.

Students are used to teachers trying to make them conform to the requirements of the marketplace (Paris & Alim, 2014). These teachers do this with goodwill, as they understand the economic and social implications of not being versed in SE. However, there is a space for teachers to have candid conversations with students about perception while helping them move between various discourse communities. We hear this echoed in Du Bois's *The Souls of Black Folk* (1903) in which he speaks of double-consciousness, and in literary works such as Langston Hughes's *I, Too, Sing America*, where he speaks of using his invisibility to grow strong and make his way to the table the next time company comes. What we *learnt* is what we always knew. AAVE is not a badge of shame, but rather an indicator of mental elasticity that breeds invention and creative and critical thought.

And Smitherman's final word sums up what is still a point of contention today: the cessation of standardized tests. As a matter of educational policy and practice, Smitherman exhorts Black English researchers: "with the support of the Black lay community, [to] push for Black language as an alternative and co-equal language of instruction. [There is] a need for public language awareness campaigns and promotion of the legitimacy of Black English" (Smitherman, 2000, p. 91). Her commentary on solutions, voiced nearly twenty years ago, still rings true.

Where are the Oakland and Ann Arbor cases of today? How can Black linguists and rhetoricians make a meaningful impact on composition pedagogy for use in urban postsecondary institutions? The history, linguistic examples, and the conversation among Black scholars about the issues presented in this text are evidence of the validity of the struggle and the persistence of the need to merge what we learned with what we learnt.

References

ACT. (2017). The condition of college of college and career readiness 2017. Retrieved from https://www.act.org/content/dam/act/unsecured/documents/cccr2017/CCCR_National_2017.pdf.

Alim, H. S., & Smitherman, G. (2012). *Articulate while Black: Barack Obama, language, and race in the U.S.* New York, NY: Oxford University Press.

Asante, K. (2005). *Race, rhetoric, and identity: The architecton of soul.* Amherst, NY: Humanity Books.

Bartholomae, D. (1986). Inventing the university. *Journal of Basic Writing, 5*(1), 4–23.

Batan, C., & Smitherman, G. (1983). White faces, Black tongues: Black English and White workers. Paper presented at the Speech Communication Association Convention, Washington, DC.

Baugh, J. (2000). *Beyond Ebonics: Linguistic pride and racial prejudices.* New York, NY: Oxford University Press.

Brookfield, S. D. (1986). *Understanding and facilitating adult learning.* San Francisco, CA: Jossey-Bass.

Campbell, K. E. (1997). "Real niggaz's don't die": African American students speaking themselves into their writing. In C. Severino, J. Guerra, & J. E. Butler (Eds.), *Writing in multicultural settings* (pp. 67–78). New York, NY: MLA.

Chesnutt, C. W. (1899). *The wife of his youth: And other stories of the color line.* Boston, MA: Houghton, Mifflin.

Chomsky, N. (1988/2004). *Language and politics.* P. Otero (Ed.). Oakland, CA: AK Press.

Conference on College Composition and Communication (CCCC). (1998, May). CCCC Statement on Ebonics. Retrieved from http://cccc.ncte.org/cccc/resources/positions/ebonics.

Darling-Hammond, L. (2004). From "separate but equal" to "no child left behind": The collision of new standards and old inequalities. In D. Meier and G. Wood (Eds.),

Many children left behind: How the No Child Left Behind Act is damaging our children and our schools (pp. 3–32). Boston, MA: Beacon Press.

———. (2005). New standards and old inequalities: School reform and the education of African American students. In J. King (Ed.), *Black education: A transformative research and action agenda for the new century* (pp. 197–224). Mahwah, NJ: Lawrence Erlbaum Associates.

Davis, K. (2012, January 12). *F*ck I Look Like!!!!* [Video file]. Retrieved from https://www.youtube.com/watch?v=hGdYAK2sLjA.

Delpit, L. (1995a). The politics of teaching literate discourse. In E. Cushman, E. Kintgen, B. Kroll, & M. Rose (Eds.), *Literacy: A critical sourcebook* (pp. 545–554). Boston, MA: Bedford/St. Martin's.

———. (1995b). *Other people's children: Cultural conflicts in the classroom.* New York, NY: The New Press.

———. (2002). *The skin that we speak: Thoughts on language and culture in the classroom.* New York, NY: The New Press.

Dillard, J. L. (1972). *Black English: Its history and usage in the United States.* New York, NY: Random House.

Du Bois, W. E. B. (1903/1994). *The souls of Black folk.* Mineola, NY: Dover Thrift.

———. (1948). The talented tenth. W. E. B. Du Bois Papers (MS 312). Special Collections and University Archives, University of Massachusetts Amherst Libraries.

Dyson, M. E. (2012). Foreword. In G. Smitherman & S. Alim, *Articulate while Black: Barack Obama, language, and race in the U.S.* (pp. ix–xiv). New York, NY: Oxford University Press.

Freire, P. (2000). *Pedagogy of the oppressed.* New York, NY: Continuum.

Fromkin, V., Rodman, R., & Hyams, N. (2002). *An introduction to language* (7th ed.). Boston, MA: Thomson.

Gee, J. P. (1989a). Literacy, discourse, and linguistics: Introduction. In E. Cushman, E. Kintgen, B. Kroll, & M. Rose (Eds.), *Literacy: A critical sourcebook* (pp. 525–537). Boston, MA: Bedford/St. Martin's.

———. (1989b). What is literacy? In E. Cushman, E. Kintgen, B. Kroll, & M. Rose (Eds.), *Literacy: A critical sourcebook* (pp. 537–544). Boston, MA: Bedford/St. Martin's.

———. (1998). Preamble to a literacy program (Unpublished document). University of Wisconsin, Madison.

———. (1999). *An introduction to discourse analysis: Theory and method.* New York, NY: Routledge.

———. (2001). Reading as situated language: A sociocognitive perspective. *Journal of Adolescent & Adult Literacy, 44,* 714–725.

———. (2004). New times and new literacies: Themes for a changing world. In A. F. Ball & S. Freedman (Eds.), *Bakhtinian perspectives on language, literacy and learning* (pp. 279–306). New York, NY: Cambridge University Press.

———. (2007). *Social linguistics and literacies: Ideology in discourses.* New York, NY: Routledge.

———. (2011). Discourse and the new literacy studies. In *Handbook of discourse analysis*. New York, NY: Routledge.
Gershenson, S., Hart, C., Lindsay, C., & Papageorge, N. W. (2017). The long-run impacts of same-race teachers. IZA Discussion Paper No. 10630, SSRN. Retrieved from https://ssrn.com/abstract=2940620.
Gilliam, W. S., Maupin, A. N., Reyes, C. R., Accavitti, M., & Shic, F. (2016). *Do early educators' implicit biases regarding sex and race relate to behavior expectations and recommendations of preschool expulsions and suspensions.* (Research Study Brief). New Haven, CT: Yale University, Yale Child Study Center.
Gilyard, K. (1999). *Race, rhetoric, and composition.* Portsmouth, NH: Boynton/Cook.
Giovanni, N. (1971). *Gemini (an extended autobiographical statement on my first twenty-five years of being a Black poet).* New York, NY: Penguin Books.
Gumperz, J. J., and Hymes, D. H. (1972). *Directions in sociolinguistics: The ethnography of communication.* New York, NY: Holt, Rinehart and Winston.
Gutierrez, K., Rymes, B., & Larson, J. (1995). Script, counterscript, and underlife in the classroom: James Brown versus Brown v. Board of Education. *Harvard Educational Review, 65*(3), 445–471.
Hassan-El, K. (1999). *The Willie Lynch letter and the making of a slave.* Bensenville, IL: Lushena Books.
Harrison, J. A. (1892). Negro English. *Modern Language Notes, 7*(2), 62.
Herskovits, Melville J. (1941). *Myth of the Negro past.* New York, NY: Harper & Brothers.
Hughes, L. (2004). "I, Too, Sing America." *The Collected Poems of Langston Hughes.* New York, NY: Vintage Books.
Hurston, Z. N. (1934/1994). The characteristics of Negro expression. In A. Mitchel (Ed.), *Within the circle: An anthology of African-American literary criticism from Harlem Renaissance to the present* (pp. 79–94). Durham, NC: Duke University Press.
———. (1977). *Talking and testifying: The language of Black America.* Boston, MA: Houghton Mifflin.
Hussar, W. J., & Bailey, T. M. (2013). *Projections of education statistics to 2022* (NCES 2014–051). U.S. Department of Education, National Center for Education Statistics. Washington, DC: U.S. Government Printing Office.
Hymes, D. (1974). *Foundations in sociolinguistics: An ethnographic approach.* Philadelphia, PA: University of Pennsylvania Press.
Johnson, K. (2014). Septima Poinsette Clark's literacy teaching approaches for linguistic acquisition and literacy development for Gullah-speaking children, 1916–1919." In Johnson, K., Pitre, A., & Johnson, K. (Eds.), *African American women educators: A critical examination of their pedagogies, educational ideas, and activism from the nineteenth to the mid-twentieth centuries* (pp. 73–106). Lanham, MD: Rowman and Littlefield Education.
Jones, T. (2014, September 19). "What is AAVE?" [Blog entry.] Retrieved from http://www.languagejones.com/?offset=1455668638435.

King, J. E. (Ed.). (2005). *Black education: A transformative research and action agenda for the new century.* Mahwah, NJ: Lawrence Erlbaum Associates.

Koss, M. K., & Williams, C. A. (2018). All American boys, #BlackLivesMatter, and Socratic seminar to promote productive dialogue in the classroom. *Illinois Reading Council Journal 46*(2), 3–15.

Labov, W. (1972). *Language in the inner city: Studies in the Black English vernacular.* Philadelphia, PA: University of Pennsylvania Press.

Labov, V., & Harris, W. A. (1986). DeFacto segregation of Black and White Vernaculars. In D. Sankoff (Ed.), *Diversity and diachrony* (pp. 1–24). Amsterdam/Philadelphia: John Benjamins.

Ladson-Billings, G. J. (1994). *The dreamkeepers: Successful teachers of African American children.* San Francisco, CA: Jossey Bass.

———. (1995). But that's just good teaching! The case for culturally relevant pedagogy. *Theory into Practice, 34*(3), 159–165.

———. (2002). I ain't writing nutting: Permissions to fail and demands to succeed in urban classrooms. In L. Delpit (Ed.), *The skin that we speak: Thoughts on language and culture in the classroom* (pp. 107–121). New York, NY: The New Press.

———. (2005). The evolving role of critical race theory in educational scholarship. *Race, Ethnicity and Education, 8*(2), 115–119.

Lee, C. D. (2007). *Culture, literacy, and learning: Taking bloom in the midst of the whirlwind.* New York, NY: Teachers College Press.

Lindquist, J., & Seitz, D. (2008). *The elements of literacy.* New York, NY: Longman.

Lipman, P. (1998). *Race and the restructuring of school.* Albany, NY: SUNY Press.

Lyiscott, J. (2014, February). *3 Ways to Speak English* [Video file]. Retrieved from https://www.ted.com/talks/jamila_lyiscott_3_ways_to_speak_english.

McWhorter, J. (1998). *Word on the street: Fact and Fable about American English.* New York: Plenum.

Mencken, H. L. (1919/1936). *The American language: An inquiry into the development of English in the United States.* New York: Knopf.

Moje, E. B. (2007). Developing socially just subject-matter instruction: A review of the literature on disciplinary literacy teaching. *Review of Research in Education, 31*(1), 1–44.

Mufweme, S. S. (2000). Some sociohistorical inferences about the development of African American English. In S. Poplac (Ed.), *The English history of African American English* (pp. 233–263). Malden, MA: Blackwell.

National Council of Teachers of English. (1974, November 30). Students' right to their own language. NCTE Annual Business Meeting, New Orleans, LA.

Nieto, S., & Bode, P. (2012). *Affirming Diversity: The sociopolitical context of multicultural education* (6th ed.). Boston, MA: Allyn and Bacon.

Oakes, J., & Lipton, M. (2007). *Teaching to change the world* (3rd ed.). Boston, MA: McGraw Hill.

Oakland Board of Education. (1996, December 18). Resolution of the Board of Education adopting the report and recommendations of the African-American Taskforce. No. 597–0063. Oakland, CA.

Paris, D. (2012). Culturally sustaining pedagogy: A needed change in stance, terminology, and practice. *Educational Researcher, 41*(3), 93–97.
Paris, D., & Alim, H. S. (2014). What are we seeking to sustain through culturally sustaining pedagogy? A loving critique forward. *Harvard Educational Review, 84*(1), 85–100.
Perry, T., & Delpit, L. (1998). *The real Ebonics debate.* Boston, MA: Beacon.
Pitre, A. (2015). *The education philosophy of Elijah Muhammad: Education for a new world* (3rd ed.). Lanham, MD: University Press of America.
Reed, C. E. (1973). Adapting TESL approaches to the teaching of written standard English as a second dialect to speakers of American Black English vernacular. *TESOL Quarterly, 7*(3), 289–307.
Rickford, J. R., & Rickford, R. J. (2000). *Spoken soul: The story of black English.* New York, NY: Wiley.
Rose, M. (1990). *Lives on the boundary.* New York, NY: Penguin.
Rosenblatt, L. M. (1994). The transactional theory of reading and writing. In R. B. Ruddell, M. R. Ruddell, & H. Singer (Eds.), *Theoretical models and processes of reading* (pp. 1057–1092). Newark, DE: International Reading Association.
Smith, E. (1997). Ebonics: The historical development of American language. San Francisco: Aspire Books.
Smitherman, G. (1977). *'Talkin' and 'testifyin': The language of Black America* (vol. 51). Detroit, MI: Wayne State University Press.
———. (1994/2000). *Black talk: Words and phrases from the hood to the amen corner.* Boston, MA: Houghton Mifflin.
———. (1995). "Students' right to their own language": A retrospective. *English Journal, 84*(1), 21–27.
———. (2000). *Talkin that talk: Language, culture and education in African America.* London: Routledge.
———. (2007). "If I'm lyin, I'm flyin": The game of insult in Black language. In L. Monaghan, J. E. Goodman, & J. M. Robinson (Eds.), *A Cultural Approach to interpersonal Communication: Essential readings* (pp. 322–330). Malden, MA: Blackwell.
Spring, J. (2006). *American education.* New York, NY: McGraw Hill.
———. (2011). *The politics of American education.* New York, NY: Routledge.
Stanovich, K. E. (2004). Matthew effects in reading: Some consequences of individual differences in the acquisition of literacy. In R. B. Rudell & N. J. Unrau (Eds.), *Theoretical models and processes of reading* (pp. 454–516). Newark, DE: International Reading Association.
Steele, C. M. (1997). A threat in the air: How stereotypes shape intellectual identity and performance. *American Psychologist, 52*(6), 613.
———. (2003). Race and the schooling of Black Americans. In S. Plous (Ed.), *Understanding prejudice and discrimination* (pp. 98–107). New York, NY: McGraw-Hill.
Stewart, W. A. (1967, 1968, in 1972) Towards a history of American Negro Dialect. In F. Williams (Ed.), *Language and poverty: Perspectives on a theme* (pp. 351–79). Chicago: Markam.

Watkins, W. (2001). *The white architects of black education: Ideology and power in America 1865–1954*. New York, NY: Teachers College Press.

Wheeler, R. S., & Swords, R. (2004). Codeswitching: Tools of language and culture transform the dialectically diverse classroom. *Language Arts, 81*(6), 470–480.

Whitney, J. (2005). Five easy pieces: Steps toward integrating AAVE into the classroom. *English Journal, 94*(5), 64–69.

Williams, C. A. (2014). *Exploring faculty beliefs regarding teaching African American freshmen to interpret social cues* (Unpublished doctoral dissertation). Northern Illinois University, DeKalb, IL.

Williams, R. (1975). *Ebonics: The true language of Black folks*. St. Louis, MO: Robert Williams and Associates.

Woodson, C. G. (2008). *The mis-education of the Negro*. Drewryville, VA: Kha Books.

Young, V. A. (2004). Your average nigga. *College Composition and Communication, 55*(4), 693–715.

Index

AAVE. *See* African American Vernacular English
Academic English, 42–47. *See also* Standard English
academic settings, AAVE in, 15–26
academic spaces, of Whites, xx–xxii
ACT Condition of College and Career Readiness report, *xix*, xix–xxii
acting White slogan, ix, xx–xxii
activities, 53–65, *57*, *58*, *61–62*
Africa, 2–3, 30
African Americans: community of, xx–xxii, 10–11; faculty as, 18–20; literacy viewed by, xv
African American students, ix–xiii, 5; college preparation of, xx, xxiv–xxvi; White students as ahead of, *xix*, xix–xxii
African American Vernacular English (AAVE), 13–26, 27–47, 49–65, *57*, *58*, *61–62*; history of, 1–11; overview of, xv, xvii–xxvi, *xix*, 67–72; unpacking of, 1–11
Africana theory of origin, 6
African genesis theory, 2–3
African Holocaust, 28
Africanisms, 2–3, 6
African Language Systems, xviii, 30
African-ness, 5

African workers, 43
Alim, H. Samy, 16–18, 46–47
American dream, xxi–xxii
American English, 3–4, 67–72
American Indian, 3, 68–69
The American Language (Mencken), 5
analysis, of discourse, 65
Anglican theory, xxii, 2, 5
Ann Arbor Decision, 9–10, 27, 72
Ann Arbor School Board, 9–10
Ann Arbor School District, 9–10
application, as activity type, 57–59, *58*
Articulate while Black (Alim and Smitherman), 46–47
ASALH. *See* Association for the Study of African American Life and History
Asante, K., xii, 8
Asian Americans, xx
aspect, 8, 42–43
assessments, 63–65
Association for the Study of African American Life and History (ASALH), xxv–xxvi

Bailey, T. M., 14
bar, 51–52
Barbados, 4

79

Bartholomae, D., 13–14
Baugh, John, 3–4, 5, 7, 11, 67–68, 69
bibliography, 60–63, *61–62*
biological linguistics, 38–39
Black Caucus, xix
Black children, reading of, 44
Black community, xx–xxii, 10–11
Black education, ix–xiii, 5
Black Education (King), xiii
Black English, xxii–xxiii, 3–11, 67–72; characteristics of, 28–29; definitions of, 32; logic and, 41–43. *See also* African American Vernacular English
Black experience, xxi
Black leaders, xii–xiii
#BlackLivesMatter, 68
Blackness, 68
Black people, ix–xiii, 4–6
Black Power, 7
Bloom's taxonomy, 53–65, *57, 58, 61–62*
Bode, P., xi
breaking process, x
Brookfield, S. D., 24
Brooklyn College, 32–47
Brown v. Board of Education of Topeka, xi

California, xxiv; Oakland in, xvii–xix, 10–11, 14, 27, 29–32, 44. *See also* Oakland Board of Education
call and response, 37–39
Caribbean, 4
Caribe Indians, 4
Catcher in the Rye (Salinger), 40–41
CCCC. *See* Conference on College Composition and Communication
"The Characteristics of Negro Expression" (Hurston), xxvi, 6, 28–29, 37–39, 46, 47
Chestnutt, Charles, 20–22
Chinese students, 39–47

Chomsky, Noam, 1–2, 5–6, 7, 10, 32, 35; on language, 38–39, 41–43, 47; Smitherman harkening back to, 71
classism, 68
classroom, AAVE in, 23–24
Clifton, Lucille, 22
code-switching, 32–47
"Cognitive and Language Development in the Black Child" (Williams), 8–10
college, 11, 15–26, 32–47; African American students prepared for, xx, xxiv–xxvi; English in, xx, 67–72
collegiate composition, AAVE partnered with, 27–47
Columbia University, 70–71
Columbus, Christopher, 3–4
Commission on Research in Black Education (CORIBE), xiii
Conference on College Composition and Communication (CCCC), xviii–xxii, *xix*
Constitution, U.S., 9–10, 30
CORIBE. *See* Commission on Research in Black Education
course syllabus information, 59–65, *61–62*
creoles, 4, 8
CSP. *See* culturally sustaining pedagogy
cultural data sets, 33–34, 43, 69
culturally sustaining pedagogy (CSP), 15

Darling-Hammond, L., xi, xii
Davis, Kai, 31
The Day Beyoncé Turned Black, 68
de-brainwashing, 32–33
deep structure, 7, 38–39, 42, 47, 71
Delpit, Lisa, xvii, xxiv, 26, 49–65
Department of Education, U.S., x
deviant model descriptor, of Black English, 6
DeVos, Betsy, 10
dialect: language or, 31–32; as Non-Standard, 70–72; as racial, 32. *See*

also African American Vernacular
  English
Dillard, J. L., 3, 4, 10, 11, 40–41,
  68–69; on Stewart, 70–71
discipline, 16
discourse: analysis of, 65; identification
  sheet of, 57–59, *58*
divergence hypothesis, 3
Dominant American English (DAE). *See*
  African American Vernacular English
Du Bois, W. E. B., xxi–xxii, 6, 11,
  44, 53, 72
Dutch, frigate of, 4
Dyson, Michael Eric, 46–47

Ebonics. *See* African American
  Vernacular English
Ebonics (Williams), 8–10
Edelin, Ramona, 9
educated Whites, 29, 67–72
education, ix–xiii, 5, 30, 68–72
EEOA. *See* Equal Education
  Opportunity Act
emancipation, 5–6
Emancipation Proclamation, 5
English: as Academic, 42–47; as
  American, 3–4; European Americans
  speaking, 1; Hurston on, 45;
  marketplace, xvii–xxvi, *xix*, 35–47,
  71–72; as pidgin, 4; SE, xx–xxvi,
  3–11, 15–26, 28–47, 67–72; slaves
  learning, 4–6; variety of, 32. *See also*
  African American Vernacular English
English-as-a-Second-Dialect
  (ESD), 32–47
English as a Second Language
  (ESL), 34–47
"The English of the Negro"
  (Krapp), 5–6
Equal Education Opportunity Act
  (EEOA), 9–10
ESD. *See* English-as-a-Second-Dialect
ESL. *See* English as a Second Language

European Americans, English
  spoken by, 1
exclusionary discipline, 16

faculty, 18–20. *See also* teachers
F*ck I Look Like!!!!, 31
first language, AAVE as, xviii
"Five Easy Pieces" (Whitney), 45
five-week assessment, 64
Flocabulary, 70
"Formation," 68
14th Amendment, 30
Freire, P., xii–xiii

gaps, xxii, 27–47, 68–72
Gee, James Paul, xxv–xxvi, 16, 49–65
Georgia, Pin Point in, 69
ghetto children, 69
gifted, and talented, tracking
  programs, xi
Giovanni, Nikki, 71
gotcha moments, 67–68
Great Migration, 5
Gullah, 69
Gutierrez, K., 23–24

Harlem Renaissance, 29
Harrison, James, 5
Harvard Civil Rights Project, xii
Heath, S. B., 50
Herskovits, Melville J., 6
Hillard, Asa, 34
Hispanic students, xi
"Holden Caulfield" (fictional
  character), 41
Holocaust, African, 28
home language, 37–47
Hughes, Langston, 72
Hurston, Zora Neale, 1, 8–10, 33–34,
  45; "The Characteristics of Negro
  Expression" by, xxvi, 6, 28–29,
  37–39, 46, 47

Hussar, W. J., 14
Hymes, Dell, 28

I, Too, Sing America (Hughes), 72
identification, 54–55, 57–59, *58*
indentured servants, 4
in-service programs and workshops, 70–71
instruction, 14–15

Jackson, Jesse, 10–11
Jim Crow, 5–6
Johnson, Karen, xii–xiii
Joiner, Charles W., 9–10
Jones, Taylor, 30–31, 33, 46

Kansas, 5
King, Joyce, xiii
King's English. *See* Standard English
Krapp, George Philip, 5–6

Labov, William, 32
Ladson-Billings, Gloria, 52
language: choices of, 54–55; Chomsky on, 38–39, 41–43, 47; or dialect, 31–32; Lee on, 41–43; in practice, 54–55; Smitherman on, 28, 29, 32, 38–39, 40, 47, 69–71; teaching of, 54–55; use of, 54–55. *See also* African American Vernacular English; English
Language of Wider Communication (LWC). *See* Standard English
Latino students, xi
Lee, Carol, xxiii, 6, 10, 33–34, 38, 69–70; on AAVE, 40; on language, 41–43
Limited English Proficiency (LEP), 30
linguistics: as biological, 38–39; Black English and, 7–11; liberation of, 67–68
Linguistics Society of America, 32
Lipman, P., xi–xii

Lipton, M., xi
literacy, xv, 49–65; social literacy, 13–26, 53–65, *57*, *58*, *61–62*
"Literacy in the Lives of African Americans," xxv–xxvi
"Liza Jane" (fictional character), 20–22
logic, Black English and, 41–43
low-track classes, xi
Lyiscott, Jamila, 31
Lynch, Willie, x

Magras, Lydia Brown, 39–47
Mann, Horace, 68
marketplace English, xvii–xxvi, *xix*, 35–47, 71–72
Martin Luther King Jr. Elementary School, 9–10
McWhorter, John, 2–3
Mencken, H. L., 5
Middle Passage, 43
migration, 5–6
miseducation, ix–xiii
"Mr. Ryder" (fictional character), 21–22
Mufweme, S. S., 2–3, 4, 5
Muhammad, Elijah, x
Myth of the Negro Past (Herskovits), 6

National Council of Teachers of English (NCTE), xviii–xxii, *xix*, 14
Native Americans, 3, 68–69
nature, 13–26
NCTE. *See* National Council of Teachers of English
Negro, 6, 28–29
Negro English (Harrison), 5
neighborhoods, of Whites, 28
NEP. *See* Non-English Proficiency
Nieto, S., xi
Niger-Congo Africa, 30
Niño, Pedro Alonzo, 3–4
No Child Left Behind Act (2001), x, xii, 44
Non-English Proficiency (NEP), 30
Non-Standard dialect, 70–72

Oakes, J., xi
Oakland, California, xvii–xix, 10–11, 14, 27, 29–32, 44
Oakland Board of Education, 10–11, 29–32, 72
Oakland Unified School District, xvii–xix, 10–11, 14, 27, 44, 72
Obama, Barack, 46–47
observation discourse map, 56–57, *57*

Paris, D., 16–18
PBI. *See* predominantly Black institution
pedagogical techniques, for AAVE speakers, 49–65, *57*, *58*, *61–62*
pickaninny, 3
pidgin English, 4
Pin Point, Georgia, 69
Pitre, Abul, xi–xiii
plantation creole, 4
"The Politics of Teaching Literate Discourse" (Delpit), 49–65
Portuguese, 3–4
PowerPoint presentation, 41
predominantly Black institution (PBI), 16–26, 59–65, *61–62*
professional standards, 60
psychological drama, 24
public education, 68–71

Race to the Top, x
racial dialect, 32
rationale, 34, 55–57, 58–59
readings: bibliography of, 60–63, *61–62*; of Black children, 44; of course, 60–63, *61–62*; Smitherman on, 44
real time, 51
Reconstruction, 5
Reed, Carol, 31–47
reflection, on activity, 55
Report No. 12 of the Massachusetts Board of Education, 68
required textbooks, 59
resolutions, 14–15

Rickford, J. R., 2–3, 7–8, 69
Rickford, R. J., 2–3, 7–8, 69
Rose, Mike, 23

St. Kitts, 4
Salinger, J. D., 40–41
sample course syllabus information, 59–65, *61–62*
"Sam Taylor" (fictional character), 20–22
Saturday Night Live, 68
saying-doing, 51–52
schedule, of course, 60
SE. *See* Standard English
second-generation segregation, xi
segregation, 5; *Brown v. Board of Education of Topeka* ending, xi; divergence hypothesis influenced by, 3; second generation of, xi
signifying, 37–39
slave masters, 4
slavery, 3
slaves, 4–6, 30, 43, 69
slave trade, 3–4
Smith, Ernie, 3
Smitherman, Geneva, 1, 3, 4, 6, 10, 24; on AAVE, 28, 31, 37–39, 43; on argument papers, 41; *Articulate while Black* by, 46–47; Chomsky harkened back to by, 71; on language, 28, 29, 32, 38–39, 40, 47, 69–71; on reading, 44; on standardized tests, 72
social literacy, 13–26, 53–65, *57*, *58*, *61–62*
The Souls of Black Folk (Du Bois), 72
South, x. *See also* segregation
speaking, 30–31, 49–65, *57*, *58*, *61–62*. *See also* African American Vernacular English
Spears, 3
special education, 30
spoken soul, 7
Spring, J., xi
Standard English (SE), xx–xxvi, 3–11, 15–26, 28–47, 67–72

standardized tests, 68, 72
Statement on Ebonics, xviii–xxii, *xix*
statements, 14–15
Steele, C. M., 22–23
Stewart, William Alexander, 70–71
students: AAVE spoken by, 13–26; as Chinese, 39–47; connecting of, 27–47; outcomes of, 59–60; teachers perceiving, 13–26, 70–72; university invented by, 13–26. *See also* African American students; White students
"Students' Right to Their Own Language" (NCTE), 14
superficial features, 52–53
Supreme Court, U.S., *Brown v. Board of Education of Topeka* ruled on by, xi
surface structure, 7, 38–39, 41–43, 71
Swords, R., 31
syllabus information, 59–65, *61–62*

"The Talented Tenth" (Du Bois), xxi–xxii
talking, xx–xxii, 22–24
teachers: AAVE perceived by, 13–26; script of, 23–24; students perceived by, 13–26, 70–72; as White, 18–20, 45
Teachers College, 70–71
teaching: AAVE and, 32–39, 49–65, *57, 58, 61–62*; of language, 54–55
ten-week assessment, 65
Test of English as a Foreign Language/ Teaching English to Speakers of Other Languages (TOEFL/ TESOL), 34–35
texts, 44–45, 46–47, 59
Thomas, Clarence, 69
TOEFL/TESOL. *See* Test of English as a Foreign Language/Teaching English to Speakers of Other Languages
trash-talking, 37–39
Turner, Lorenzo Dow, 6

university, 11, 13–26

variety of English, 32. *See also* Black English
Virginia, Africans brought to, 4

Watkins, W., x
West Africa, 2–3, 8, 30
Wheeler, R. S., 31
whiteness, SE aligned with, 19–20
Whites: academic spaces of, xx–xxii; acting, ix, xx–xxii; Asante on, xii; as educated, 29, 67–72; faculty as, 18–20; institutions of, 43–47; neighborhoods of, 28; slave masters, 4; Smitherman on, 10; teachers as, 18–20, 45; world of, 53. *See also* Standard English
White students, xi; African American students as behind, *xix*, xix–xxii; SE aligned with, 19; talking of, 22; writing of, 22
White supremacy, xi
Whitney, Jessica, 44, 45–46
The Wife of His Youth (Chestnutt), 20–22
Williams, Robert, 8–10
will to adorn, 1, 29, 33–34
Woodson, Carter G., x, 6
workers, 43
writing, 22–24

Young, V. A., 23–24, 52

About the Authors

Concetta A. Williams is an assistant professor of English at Chicago State University. She earned her EdD in literacy education with a focus on postsecondary literacy and literacy transitions from Northern Illinois University, and she also holds an MA degree in literature and an MAT degree in secondary English education. Her experience includes teaching at the primary, secondary, and postsecondary levels, and she has spent much of her teaching career in urban settings. Dr. Williams's research focuses on broadening the definition of literacy in an effort to better understand perceptions of literate behavior in academic settings, reconceptualizing literacy as a social practice, using literacy as means of developing social capital, and working with diverse student populations (first-year, first-generation).

Lydia Magras received her PhD in English from Purdue University. Her dissertation focused on aspects of spirituality in the works of twentieth-century American women writers. Dr. Magras also holds a Master of Social Work degree from the University of Illinois, Urbana-Champaign, where she completed her undergraduate work in English. She has taught composition and African American literature at Muhammad University of Islam in Chicago, City Colleges of Chicago, Chicago State University, and Purdue University.

Dr. Magras is the author of "Popular Reception of Toni Morrison's *Beloved*: Reading the Text through Time" (*Reception,* 7[1], 2015) and "Identity and Worldview" in *The Encyclopedia of Identity*, edited by Ronald L. Jackson (2010). She also has served as a reviewer for *MELUS* and as a contributing columnist to the *Final Call* newspaper.

Dr. Magras has presented her research before the National Council of Black Studies; the Association for the Study of African American History and

Life; the Elijah Muhammad Studies Research Symposium; the Conference of Religion, Literature, and the Arts; Reception Studies Society; and the American Literature Association.

Her research interests include urban and cultural literacies, spirituality and literature, and women's literature. Her current project focuses on literacy and Elijah Muhammad.

www.ingramcontent.com/pod-product-compliance
Lightning Source LLC
Chambersburg PA
CBHW032030230426
43671CB00005B/262